COMPENDIUM OF NORTH AMERICAN CRYPTIDS & MAGICAL CREATURES

OFFICIAL GUIDE OF THE

MAGIMUNDI™

COMPENDIUM OF NORTH AMERICAN CRYPTIDS & MAGICAL CREATURES

OFFICIAL GUIDE OF THE

MAGIMUNDI™

By Foxfire Castellaw

Annotated by Wyn Diego

150th Anniversary Edition, updated with new creatures

Approved for use in education by the

Magimundi Bureau of Wizard Training & Tutelage

Written by Mike Young, Maury Brown and Ben Morrow

Illustrated by Ffion Evans

Published in the United States by Inexorable Media.

SECOND EDITION

Library of Congress Cataloging-in-Publication Data
Young, Mike 1966-
Brown, Maury 1969-
Morrow, Ben 1976-
Evans, Ffion, ill. 1989-

Compendium of North American Cryptids & Magical
Creatures / Mike Young, Maury Brown and Ben Morrow.

ISBN-10:1-945097-00-0
ISBN-13:978-1-945097-00-3

www.learnlarp.com
www.magischola.com
www.magimundi.wiki

Book Design by Erica Schoonmaker
Cover Design by Anna Kovatcheva
Foxfire Castellaw portrait by Lars Bundvad

To Laura – M.Y.

*To my grandmother, Eleanor Volpinari Palumbo, and to Willow,
Austin & Maria, magical beings, all. And to Ben, of course. – M.B.*

*To Allan and Madonna Morrow, and to Maury,
the best is yet to come. – B.M.*

The authors would like to thank: Erica Schoonmaker, Maddy Wojdak, Toivo Voll, Marie Del Rio, Kathryn Lieber, David Neubauer, Tara Clapper, Sarah Brand, Rhiannon Chiacchiaro, Suzanne Molloy, Lee Parmenter, Anna Yardney, Anna Kovatcheva, Anne Serup Grove, Lars Bundvad, Browning Porter, Ffion Evans, Rob Balder, Linda Paolino, and all the backers, fans, and supporters of a new world of magic for North America.

Dedication to the 150th Anniversary Edition

Wyn Diego

Gone, but not forgotten.

1919-2016

This book is dedicated to the entrepreneur, adventurer, cryptozoologist, and erstwhile scholar, Wyn Diego. Shortly after turning in the annotations for this book, Wyn disappeared while on an expedition with Virginia Isle Traders. It has now been several months, and as no one has heard from him, he is presumed dead. It appears that Wyn's last words may be those found within this Compendium.

Though well-beloved by the general public for his gripping accounts of journeys to the bottom of the sea to locate the lair of the Lightning Snakes or into the air to document the nests of the Thunderbird, Wyn was not always popular in scientific and regulatory circles. He was opinionated and honest to a fault. You never had to guess where you stood with Wyn: if he thought something, he said it. We always said he lacked any restrictions of decorum, but others called it a lack of good breeding, good taste, and good upbringing. Still others were certain that he must have been suffering from a magical ailment, which— while there is no evidence to corroborate this notion—is entirely plausible given his profession and propensity for staring danger in the face and overcoming it with unique and unconventional means. If Wyn is dead, and sadly we must admit that to be the case, then he died by the code he lived by, which, we suppose, is as good a death as any of us can imagine for ourselves.

TABLE OF CONTENTS

About the Author

Foxfire Castellaw suffered from having a rather poor memory. Rather than allow this to inhibit his abilities as a wizard or cryptozoologist, Foxfire instead created what began as a rudimentary filing system by means of enchanting sheets of parchment and creating an artifact charcoal pencil. As it turned out, Foxfire had a gift for organization and description, and his filing system became the first edition of the "Compendium of Local Creatures." As is known to all, the compendium was a breakthrough, sorting out all the apocryphal information from what Foxfire referred to as "the good stuff." The compendium's readers demanded an expanded edition, and so Foxfire began his tour of the Magimundi to document the various cryptids and magical creatures. The old man is no longer with us, but the end of his life was happy, knowing that his "little book" inspired so many cryptozoologists. This edition of the *Compendium* features as much of Foxfire's original text as possible, with the help of contributors to fill in the gaps or update with new or changed information.

FOREWORD

by Foxfire Castellaw

Hello. Thank you for electing to take a bit of your time to read my little book. I apologize for being a bit verbose from time to time. I've tried to keep the reading down to a minimum, and deliver the relevant information as concisely as possible. That said, the book is too long, and I'd really like to get it down to even less, but folks have been telling me that the book is just fine, and they may be telling the truth rather than just trying to stop me from making yet another edit so they can send it to the publisher. I never saw myself as a writer of books, just someone who himself benefitted from having good, useful information handy when it was needed. So that's what this was. But I am very happy to know that enough other people found this information handy as well, enough so that they'd buy it. It's a strange thing. If my older brother were alive, and I told him, "Oh by the way, I have become a writer," he would most likely reply, "What in the devil do you know enough of to write down to fill two pages, let alone a whole book, and what would make anybody with a sound mind want to read what you think you know?" Well, Ignatius Castellaw, my older brother, though I love you as family should and must, you were wrong about me, needlessly unkind to everyone else around you too, and finally dead and buried in your own grave due to your own stupidity and arrogance. So, how do you like them apples, Iggy? I seem to have wandered from the central topic once again. Please excuse me. What I mean to say is that I thank you for reading, and I hope that you find the book useful and informative. If you discover any new information, or maybe just something that I have missed, please do send me a letter with as much detail and documentation as possible, so I can improve this work. While I did perform a lot of the work of the writing of this book, the fact is that I met many different and wonderful people who were there to provide me with all sorts of help, not just information, but to bring me around where they live and show me the things that needed to be seen. I do not believe I have another tour of the Provinces in me, but your letters and drawings and correspondence are of great help. Now this introduction is too long. I humbly apologize. Please take care.

INTRODUCTION TO THE MAGIMUNDI

In North America, the concealed magical world is known as the Magimundi. The Magimundi is highly organized and is comprised of five provinces: Destiny (Northeast US and Eastern Canada), Solaris (Southeast US and Caribbean), Baja (Southwest US, Mexico, and Central America), Thunderbird (Pacific Northwest US and Western Canada), and Mishipeshu (Midwest US and mid-Canada). Each of these Provinces is governed by an Arch Justice. The five Arch Justices of each region together form The Council of Five who serve as the highest court and governing body of the North American magical world. Under the Arch Justices are Regional Justices who appoint Magisters, who oversee North American Magical Agencies (such as the Magister of Metallurgy who oversees each province's mines of magical ore), or the governing of a province itself (such as the General Magister of Solaris Province who handles the day-to-day governing of the province on behalf of its Justice). Magisters appoint ranks of other provincial officials who are responsible for all official matters in the region. These officials are known as Alcalde in the Solaris and Baja regions and Fonctionnaires in the other regions. The Alcalde and Fonctionnaires directly interface with the rest of the Magimundi.

There are a few areas that operate independently of the Provinces. The cities in Alaska and the northern areas of Canada are neighborly to the Thunderbird Province and connected by commerce but not under direct Provincial control. Likewise, the further south into Central America, the less influence the Baja Province has over the lives of the magical communities there. Perhaps most interesting is Virginia Isle—

the floating island said to have been lifted into the air out of the sea by the magic of Virginia Dare herself, which is entirely autonomous.

Each province has a magical primary school, listed briefly below:

- **Destiny Province**: Providence Preparatory Academy for the Advancement of the Arcane Arts (P2A4)
- **Solaris Province**: Magnolia Sun School of Sorcery
- **Mishipeshu Province**: Great Plains School of Magical Arts
- **Thunderbird Province**: Lewis & Clark Institute of Magic
- **Baja Province**: Flower Mountain Escuela Mágico

The common currency of the Provinces is the Leeuwendaalder, and any family's liquid worth in Leeuwendaalders significantly impacts that family's status and prosperity. Magi from otherwise mundane families that exhibit magical prowess are severely disadvantaged by their family's lack of Leeuwendaalders and are often only able to succeed with help from philanthropic organizations that provide patronage until they graduate, conditional to their academic performance. The unlucky individuals that receive no assistance or intervention have to find the means to fund their education all on their own, literally starting out with nothing at all.

People who manifest magical powers become members of the Magimundi and are known as magi until they earn the title of Wizard by completing Magischola. Note: all people who have mastered the art of wielding arcane powers are known as wizards, regardless of gender. 'Wizard' is an official title earned by those who have completed Magischola. Those without such a credential may be known as magi or as sorcerers but not wizards. Again, mage and sorcerer are used regardless of gender.

In North America, the official, accredited magical colleges are known as Magischola. There are currently two fully accredited Magischolae, though some others are in the process of seeking accreditation. These are Imperial Magischolae of Massachusetts Bay, located in Destiny Province, and New World Magischola in Solaris. Only a credentialed graduate of an accredited Magischola can be considered an actual Wizard in the provinces and seek corresponding employment.

This book is used by all students at New World Magischola, where one of the Wizard paths students may follow is a specialization in Cryptozoology. Cryptozoology, as a scholarly discipline, was established in 1635 with the creation of New World Magischola by House Croatan founder Virginia Dare, who possessed an extraordinary ability to communicate with magical creatures and dedicated much of her resources to providing for their care and conservation. Prior to Dare's introduction of the field to Magischola, knowledge about magical creatures was typically passed down through tutorial sessions within groups of magic users.

AN INTRODUCTION TO CRYPTOZOOLOGY

This is the first and last time that the author will say something both useful and accurate in this text. That is of course, why I, Wyn Diego, the renowned adventurer and foremost modern expert on Cryptozoology, have been invited by the Publisher to annotate this piece of work.

Cryptozoology is the study of magical creatures. It includes, in particular, those creatures generally known as cryptids whose existence has not been scientifically substantiated by the Mundane world. Of course not, we say! Since these are inherently magical creatures, their existence is unknown to Mundanes, and even when there are reported sightings, their community is quick to discredit the eye-witnesses (a well-timed *Muta Memoria* spell may also have something to do with keeping these creatures' existence secret, but more on that later). Some Mundanes know of certain cryptids and creatures from legends and stories told at their camps and slumber parties. Their versions of these cryptids are often quite quaint, and we in the Magimundi do not attempt to correct their misperceptions. Part of our job is to preserve and protect these creatures, which means keeping them safe from the eyes and ears—and weapons and wallets—of Mundane scientists, poachers, and curiosity-seekers.

The study of cryptozoology includes anatomy, ecology, and conservation. In this guide, you will learn how to recognize and approach a magical creature and to understand its habitat, diet, biology, and behavior. A knowledgeable Wizard and wizard-in-training also knows how to care for and defend against a creature, in addition to knowing the practical uses any magical beast can offer—either alive (such as a means of transportation or a companion) or dead (such as for use as food or in wands, potions, charms, rituals, and other types of magic).

Understanding the behavior of cryptids and magical creatures is important, as this knowledge can improve the lives of both the creatures and Magimundi. One example can be seen in the chupacabra of the Yellowstone Caldera. These creatures were dying out in the wild, but after being domesticated by the Magimundi, chupacabra are thriving and now perform many valuable tasks as well as provide a source of very useful magical components.

Blah blah blah blah. Categorizing is nice for people who like to put things into lists, but it's arbitrary enough to be useless. Cryptozoological creatures are, themselves, all unique cases, and they resist accurate categorization. The nuances are what counts, and that's actually the kind of information that's lost in these silly lists. If your Cryptozoology professor asks a question about a creature's classification, be sure to answer the question by saying, "Arbitrary categorization might have been acceptable to backwoods ignoramuses, but in the modern era it's rightly defined as a retreat from genuine knowledge of the subject matter," and then tell them Wyn Diego said so.

THE CLASSIFICATION OF MAGICAL BEINGS

In order to distinguish between the different magical beings as well as to group them by similar characteristics, a series of classifications has been established and agreed upon by the Magimundi Council of Five. These categories are very important as magical laws, policies, and regulations are created to support them. Restrictions on what may be harvested, when, by whom, and how often are formed as a result of the research and recommendations of cryptozoologists, and this guide uses the official designations and rulings set down by the Council.

This guide uses four different systems of classification: **Latin**, **Sapience**, **Manifestation**, and **Family**.

The **Latin** classification describes the properties of a creature and helps connect similar species. Latin classifications are included to foster further study of the subject and to align with Mundane taxonomy practices. Latin has a long history of being used in the sciences as a *lingua franca*, and these classifications help Wizards and magi from around the world compare and categorize creatures.

The most complex classification is **Sapience**, which includes four designations: **Sapient**, **Non-sapient**, **Semi-Sapient** and **Para-Sapient**. This classification explains whether a creature has the ability of self-reflection and is capable of understanding moral and ethical reasoning. Beings with these abilities are called sapient creatures. Any creature lacking these characteristics is classified as non-sapient. Non-sapient creatures can sometimes behave like sapient creatures, but since they are governed by instincts and cannot reflect on their actions, they are not sapient. Creatures can be called semi-sapient if they seem to exhibit sapience in some scenarios but not always. This category may also be used if the status of the creature is in dispute in magi-academic circles. Creatures with a non-human or otherworldly understanding of morals and ethics are called para-sapient and appear to be capable of a sort of self-reflection, though any system of morals and values they may possess does not correlate with that of human beings. This classification is the subject of much debate in the field of Cryptozoology and Magical Jurisprudence.

Manifestation is used to classify how a creature presents itself in and interacts with the physical world. Creatures may be classified as **corporeal**, **spectral**, or, in rare cases, **phasic**. A corporeal being has mass, can touch and be touched, and directly interacts with the physical world. Spectral beings are apparitions that can be perceived using one or more of the senses, but do not have mass and cannot directly interact with the physical world. Phasic beings may change between corporeal and spectral in accordance with their will or circumstances.

Family allows for a basic grouping of creatures by traits or habitat. A listing of the Families of magical creatures follows.

FAMILIES

That would explain the author, wouldn't it? But sadly, no, the author has been verified to have been a mortal Wizard whose mental deficiencies are all his own.

ANIMATA: These creatures tend to be non-sapient constructs created by magi or by natural magic. It is possible for some animata creatures to gain para-sapience through magical means. Both homunculi and golems are examples of creatures from the animata family.

ARBOREAL: Creatures in the arboreal family look and behave like plants, but many are sapient or para-sapient. There is considerable debate between the cryptozoologists and the parabotanists as to the true category of arboreal beings as both sides would like to lay claim.

AVERINE: The averine family is defined by their birdlike characteristics. An averine creature has feathered wings but does not need the ability to fly in order to qualify. Nesting and roosting are also common denominators for all averine creatures, all of which lay eggs with hard shells and care for their young.

CHIMERICAL: Chimeras are creatures that are seemingly comprised of parts of other creatures. Sometimes these creatures seem to be from different families; in which case, they are listed with the complete familial classification.

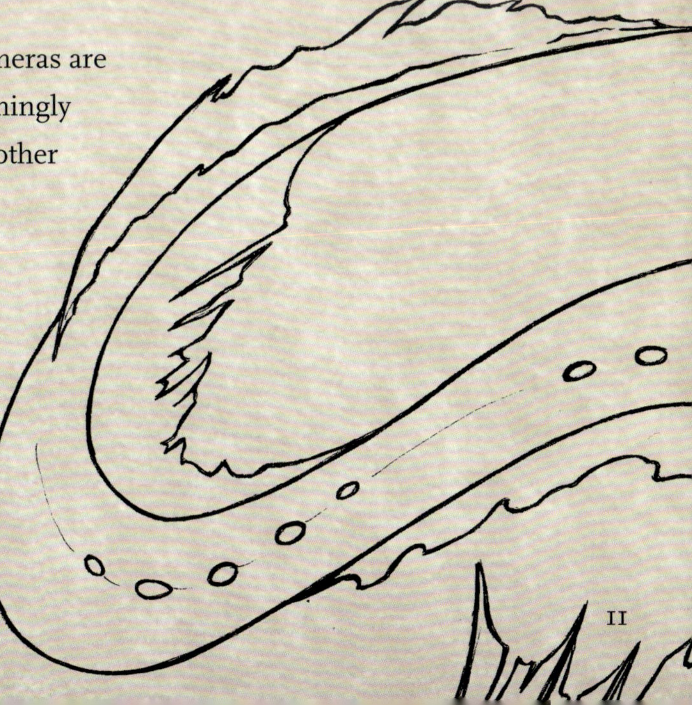

HUMANOID: The humanoid family includes all human-like creatures that are neither nemort (undead) nor spirit. They are either completely human in appearance or share the most noticeable human traits such as an upright posture and human head, hands, and feet. Most humanoids are sapient or para-sapient but exceptions exist. Many humanoids are also mammalian but not always.

ICHTHYOLIOS: Members of the Ichthyolios family have piscine (fishlike) qualities and live in bodies of fresh or salt water. Ichthyoids tend to be cold-blooded, with the noticeable exception of the Mermaid.

INSECTOID: The family of insectoids are cold-blooded creatures with more than four legs and compound eyes. Insectoids lay eggs with a soft shell. This family includes arachnid (spider-like) creatures as well as coleoptera (beetle) and muscidae (fly-like) ones.

Arachnids are not insects. Everyone knows this. But hey, "insectoid" means like an insect, so I guess you are sort of like an insect if you have eight legs instead of six. But then, an octopus and a cuttlefish have eight "legs," by which we mean tentacles or arms; and well, the argument enters reducto ad absurdum. So, we can just pretend not to know these things and include arachnids with the Insectoid family. Whatever.

MAMMALIAN: This family contains a large number of varied species. These creatures are warm-blooded, covered in hair, and nurse their young.

NEMORT: The Nemort family is comprised both of undead and reanimated creatures, few of which display typical signs of life such as heartbeat, breathing, and electrical or magical currents in the body (vampires are a notable exception). Nemorts are created or born from the body and/or soul of a creature previously alive. The vast majority of undead creatures are non-sapient; however, some such as vampires and liches (see revenant) are para-sapient.

REPTILIAN: Members of the reptilian family are usually covered in scales of some sort. They are cold-blooded creatures who often prefer to settle in dark, damp places. Reptiles lay eggs and then usually leave the young to fend for themselves, with the exception of dragons who care for their young. *There are no dragons native to the Americas.*

SPIRIT: Spirit creatures can be recognized by their connection to the spirit realm. They differ from the undead in that the undead have a physical body, while the spirit creatures tend to be spectral or, in rare cases, phasic.

Ahuizotl

Ahuizotl aqua

FAMILY: *Mammalian*
CLASSIFICATION: *Non-sapient*
MANIFESTATION: *Corporeal*
PRONUNCIATION: *ah-wē-ZOH-tul*

The ahuizotl is a small dog-like magical creature prevalent in the Baja Province. It has dexterous paws and a fully articulated hand on its tail, which it uses to snatch its prey, dragging it into the depths to drown it.

An ahuizotl is a mammal and breathes air. It has the ability to hold its breath submerged in the water for hours so it can better stalk its prey.

Ahuizotl live near bodies of water. There are river and lake varieties of ahuizotl and, while they prefer fresh water, they can adapt to salt water if necessary. They prefer to hunt via submerged capture but they are able to survive on land during dry spells. In this case, they will use their tail-hand to snatch their prey, holding it down with the front paws; a bite to the neck will usually finish the kill. In rare instances ahuizotl will scavenge by following a pack of coyotes and sharing their meals.

The ahuizotl has the ability to mimic distress calls of a variety of young animals, including human infants. Ahuizotls use this cry to lure their prey to the banks of the water where they then snatch the victim, pull them in and drown them.

Ahuizotls live in a pack with a dominant female, her mate and their pups, though ahuizotl have been known to adopt orphans and stragglers from other packs as well. A grown ahuizotl is about the size of a small dog.

A juvenile ahuizotl is called a pup. The collective noun for a group of ahuzoitls is a pack.

HABITAT: Ahuizotls live mainly in Baja Province near lakes and rivers. They can survive dry spells as scavengers but prefer to hunt for prey.

BIOLOGY: Ahuizotls are aquatic mammals and have a special bladder that they can use to store air and survive underwater for up to four hours. They have raccoon-like hands instead of paws as well as a fifth, fully articulated, human-like hand on the end of their tail. The fur of the ahuizotl has a blue sheen and is rubbery, water resistant, and clumps easily, forming spikes. They are carnivores. They require high amounts of keratin and calcium in their diet so they tend to consume the nails and teeth of their victims first before moving on to the soft tissue.

If you can stand the smell! Who wants to stink like a wet dog?

MAGICAL USES: Ahuizotl fur may be woven into water-resistant clothing. The fur can be used as the cores of wands and their fingernails can enhance water- and grasping-based powers to a wand. Their air bladders can be fashioned into a magical mask that allows the wearer to survive underwater without air for four hours. Their assorted other organs can be used as components in potions and charms.

DEFENSE: The success of an ahuizotl hunt is dependent upon the effectiveness of its cries as a lure, and any mage with a certain amount of pragmatic callousness may be too wary to investigate the sound. But should a cautious mage approach a body of water, wary of the ahuizotl, any of the various water-breathing magics will at least be helpful. However, an ahuizotl pack will not simply abandon a prey that fails to drown in the expected manner, and can outwait the water-breathing magic or simply render enough damage with their teeth that breathing underwater becomes a moot point. Aside from such drastic efforts such as evaporating, freezing, or turning the body of water to acid (creating other problems for the Wizard), it's suggested that a Wizard underwater and attacked by Ahuizotl select the largest of the pack, and gouge its eyes out with fingers or teeth. With the leader wounded the pack has been observed to withdraw, however this is known to be a long shot since an unprepared Wizard is quite often a dead Wizard.

The Ahuizotl are trying to consume your fingernails, and you suggest putting your hands towards its face? Perhaps you'd also suggest cutting your own arm off and making a peace offering with it? No. These creatures are basically wild dogs and about as intelligent. A bag of teeth dumped into the water will keep them occupied for days, they will even keep searching the water's bottom long after the teeth have been consumed for a hidden extra. No teeth? Collect your party's fingernail clippings, and that will serve also for distraction long enough to make a getaway.

CACTUS CAT

Felis cactaceae

FAMILY: *Arboreal*
CLASSIFICATION: *Non-sapient*
MANIFESTATION: *Corporeal*
PRONUNCIATION: *KAK-tus/KAT*

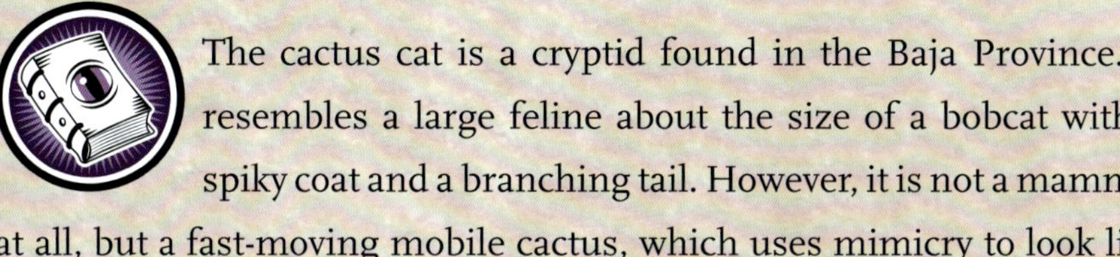

The cactus cat is a cryptid found in the Baja Province. It resembles a large feline about the size of a bobcat with a spiky coat and a branching tail. However, it is not a mammal at all, but a fast-moving mobile cactus, which uses mimicry to look like a cat.

The cactus cat does not put down roots. It obtains nutrients by slashing open normal cacti and drinking the sap, often waiting a day or two for the sap to ferment. Drinking heavily of this mezcal-like substance will intoxicate the cactus cat, which will then dance, stumble around, and make loud yowling sounds through the night.

Cactus cats are green and can photosynthesize but still require the sap of local cacti for nutrients. They have four feet, with razor-sharp claws, as well as a traditional cat's face, with eyes, ears, a nose, a mouth, and spiky whiskers. These all seem to perform the same sensory functions as they do with an actual cat, allowing the cactus cat to see, hear, and smell, and use the whiskers for balance and sizing. They do not appear to have any sense of taste.

Cactus cats do not breathe as mammals do, but "inhale" carbon dioxide and "exhale" oxygen as part of photosynthesis. They are able to vocalize and their drunken night caterwauling is a memorable experience. They can also purr.

Cactus cats do not have typical mammalian internal organs but possess a spongy interior similar to a cactus. They do not seem to feel pain, but dislike and will resist being cut. Cactus cats also have an internal sap which is highly alcoholic and magical. Cactus cat sap (colloquially called "cat juice" or "catsap") is supposed to be able to get one pleasantly drunk with just one sip; however, it causes a wicked hangover the next morning. It is a magical hangover, immune to all charms and attempts to dispel it.

Yet more evidence of the true goals of the author: drunkenness.

Both male and female cactus cats will flower in the late summer. The flowers appear around the neck or head area of the cat and can give the appearance of wearing a hat, brooch, or pendant. Cactus cat flowers are usually dark red, pink, or purple and have a pleasant scent with a touch of mezcal.

Cactus cats live in family groups in the wild, with both male and female alternating as leaders. Once the cactus kittens mature, they leave to form their own family groups. Cactus cats are fiercely protective of their space and mark their territory with scent. However, cactus cats from many different territories are known to congregate when drunk for a group yowl.

Cactus cats can be kept as pets, and much like their mammalian counterparts they enjoy resting in the sunlight and destroying houseplants. They cannot be trained, although they can be used as familiars. Their flowers can be harvested both as spell and alchemy components and as decoration.

A juvenile cactus cat is called a cactus kitten. The collective noun for a family of cactus cats is a family. Groups larger than a family are called a cacophony.

I have invented a particularly effective potion that can indeed dispel the effects of a catsap hangover, pending approval by the Bureau of Alchemical Ingredients and Reagents Controls. I always have some available after my private parties, should you find yourself invited. Take at your own risk, of course.

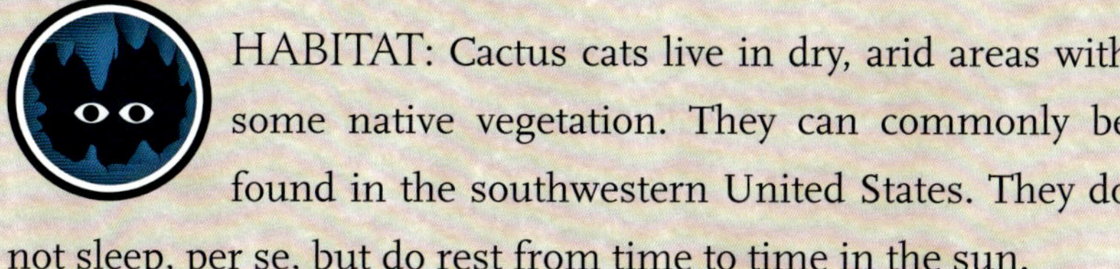

HABITAT: Cactus cats live in dry, arid areas with some native vegetation. They can commonly be found in the southwestern United States. They do not sleep, per se, but do rest from time to time in the sun.

BIOLOGY: Internally, cactus cats resemble the cacti they feed from however, they do have sensory organs on their face and a mass of tissue in the head area resembling a brain. They have sharp, retractable claws, and spines on their "pelt." Cactus cats reproduce sexually via pollination of a female cat's flowers.

DIET: Cactus cats photosynthesize and also drink the sap of native cacti. They do not drink each other's sap.

MAGICAL USES: The spines of cactus cats may occasionally be used for wands. Their flowers can be used in charms and ground into potions. Their sap can be used in potions as well, or drunk as a powerful alcoholic beverage. Cactus cats may be kept as pets or used as familiars. The sensory organs of cactus cats may be used in spells that require similar sensory organs, eyes for eyes and so forth, but they produce unpredictable results.

WRONG.

DEFENSE: Cactus cats typically do not attack unless defending their young and they have no natural fear of humans, often choosing to simply ignore those who pass through (as long as they keep moving). The chief weapons of the cactus cat are its razor-sharp claws and teeth and its spiked tail. Its spiny coat grants it an excellent defense against most physical attacks, and it is only vulnerable to plant (rather than animal) spells. The best way to befriend a cactus cat is to carry a flask of liquor, the closer to mezcal or tequila the better. Drawn by the scent, cactus cats will actively come to you, drink the liquor and allow themselves to be petted and scratched. Watch out for the spines when you pet them.

The modern era has either seen a change in the Cactus cat or the author's information is out of date. Cactus cats are FAR greater in population today than previously believed, and packs of them will find you and take any and all alcohol by force. They've also got this clever trick of sending one cat in for the friendly approach, and as soon as the alcohol comes out, the whole army of them are suddenly insisting that you share all of it.

CHUPACABRA

Hircum potator

FAMILY: *Reptilian*
CLASSIFICATION: *Semi-Sapient*
MANIFESTATION: *Corporeal*
PRONUNCIATION: *CHŪ-pe-CA-bruh*

The chupacabra (also known as "Goat Sucker") is a large reptile inhabiting a wide territory of the Americas, though it prefers warmer climes, especially near Central America and the southwestern United States. The name comes from the creature's habit of attacking and drinking the blood of livestock, especially goats. It has also been known to attack satyrs and fauns. In a single reported case, a swarm of chupacabra took down a full-grown wampus cat.

It is a heavy creature, easily the size of a small bear, with a row of spines descending from the neck to the base of the tail. It has a smooth light green skin with darker spots and large, black eyes. The chupacabra has a venomous bite which can cause death in a human being.

Chupacabra exist in the wild, but following the Magma Wars of the 1800s, their numbers were extremely reduced. They are only recently beginning to rebound in the wild. They thrive in domestication with some chupacabra ranches reaching over 3,000 head. Chupacabra are highly aggressive and are not kept as family pets or familiars; however, they can be trained as guard creatures, or to attack on command. Chupacabra are used to guard the Avernus prison in the Yellowstone Caldera. Wild chupacabra are noticeably larger than their domesticated cousins.

The chupacabra is a quite intelligent animal, able to solve simple problems, be trained, and even mimic human speech as parrots do (a form of echolalia). Because of this, there is a push in the magical community to change their classification to para-sapient, though they have shown no signs of having a sense of self or ability to act on anything but instinctual, animalistic behavior. They are still officially considered semi-sapient by the Bureau of Cryptozoological Resources as of the Edict of Classification of Creatures.

A juvenile chupacabra is called a hatchling. Female chupacabra usually lay 5-7 eggs at time. The collective noun for a group of chupacabra is a swarm.

HABITAT: Chupacabra used to thrive in the Baja Province but were culled during the Magma Wars. The wild chupacabra is on the rebound now.

BIOLOGY: Chupacabra are lizards with sharp claws, pointed teeth and a venomous bite. They walk upright. They are carnivorous, preferring small to medium livestock such as goats and sheep. Adult chupacabra have been known to prey on cattle as well, leading to rumors among mundane ranchers of cattle mutilators from outer space.

MAGICAL USES: Chupacabra spines may be used as wands. Their teeth, eyes, and internal organs may be used for potions, charms, and fetishes. Their venom is quite toxic, and although an anti-venom has been developed, like all anti-venoms it requires fresh venom to create. Chupacabra meat is edible and is considered a gourmet treat. It has a slightly fishy taste but with the consistency of chicken.

DEFENSE: By the Edict of Avernus Security, defense against Chupacabra is considered to be privileged information, and has been redacted.

Note: Wyn Diego's original commentary has been redacted.

Since my commentary on the chupacabra defense has been redacted, I will simply state that I am available for private consulting sessions at reasonable rates.

DUWENDE

Lux volant

DUWENDE

FAMILY: *Spirit*
CLASSIFICATION: *Non-sapient*
MANIFESTATION: *Spectral*
PRONUNCIATION: *dū-WEN-dā*

The duwende is a tiny luminous fae creature, cousin to the European Will O' The Wisp, and are as likely to lead a traveller astray as guide them to safety. Duwenden congregate in underground caverns and water passageways in the American and Canadian Midwest and will likely be familiar to students at Great Plains School of the Magical Arts as they make their way to the school each fall.

Duwenden live in colonies beneath the earth and only leave their cavern in times of crisis and to swarm. Duwenden colonies have an eusocial hierarchy and colonies consist of sterile females forming castes of "workers," "soldiers," or other specialized groups, some fertile males called "drones," and one or more fertile females called "queens."

Most encounters with a duwende are with the worker-class, which are mischievous but harmless. The soldiers and queens can attack and cause blindness, first degree burns, and a strange condition where the victim is unable to use any magical powers that enhance vision. This magical blindness is usually temporary, but in rare cases can be permanent.

Duwende colonies can grow to as large as 2,000 to 5,000 duwenden. Duwende swarming occurs naturally as a result of overcrowding within a cavern. During a swarm, an old queen leaves the colony with about half of the colony's workers, while a new queen remains in the cavern with the rest of the workers. Duwenden swarm most in late spring and early summer, exactly at midnight. The sight has been described as breathtaking.

A duwende is able to glow at birth. Duwenden produce a sort of ectoplasm (colloquially known as "the goo") which they store for food. Usually a pale green, glowing liquid, it can be other colors if the colony is unhealthy. If duwenden are attacked, they can "pop" which sprays the ectoplasm on their attackers.

Ectoplasm can permanently stain fabrics. Do not wear your best shirt.

HABITAT: Duwenden dwell in caves and caverns in the midwestern United States and Canada.

BIOLOGY: A duwende appears as a small pale green sphere internally illuminated by a swirling glow. It produces an ectoplasm which can be concentrated into a weapon.

DIET: Duwenden survive on ectoplasm created by draining the life force out of plants outside their caves. The process of draining does not kill the plant, but has been known to retard its growth and rate of photosynthesis. Duwende are also known to feed on the life force of mosses and molds within their caverns.

MAGICAL USES: Ectoplasm is a powerful magical ingredient and can be concentrated into a weapon. Some magi farm duwenden and use them to light their underground chambers. There are spells that can use duwenden to carry messages great distances. Duwenden possess a sort of homing instinct that allows them to return to their queen regardless of where they are.

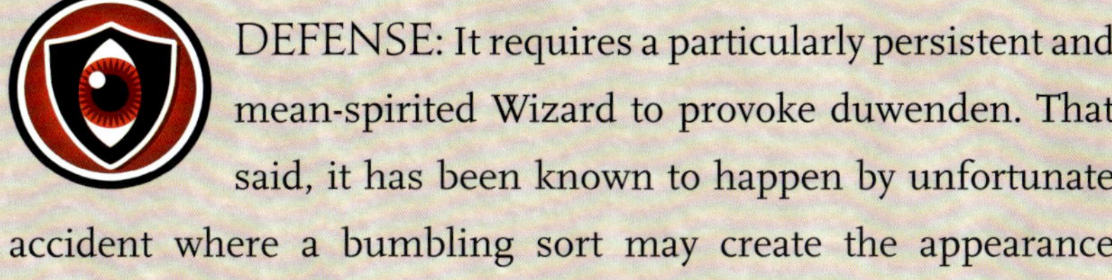

DEFENSE: It requires a particularly persistent and mean-spirited Wizard to provoke duwenden. That said, it has been known to happen by unfortunate accident where a bumbling sort may create the appearance of aggression toward the duwende Queen. Any individual duwende can safely be ignored, but a swarm will require the Wizard to have suitable eye protection at the ready. A lightning spell is the best defense against a duwende swarm, as it causes a chain-reaction of explosions among them, leaving a puddle of ectoplasm behind. For more widespread extermination, introducing skree lichen to their environment will eventually poison their ectoplasm and wipe out the infestation.

Attempts to weaponize the surge and explosion have gone poorly. Don't do it, trust me.

FAIRYMAID

Samodiva america

FAMILY: *Humanoid*
CLASSIFICATION: *Para-sapient*
MANIFESTATION: *Phasic*
PRONUNCIATION: *FĀR-ē-MĀD*

Fairymaids are beautiful creatures with long lush hair, feathered wings (which may or may not be visible), and one tiny foot in the shape of a deer's hoof. Like the *Wila* or *Samodiva* of Europe, they are usually dressed in free-flowing gowns decorated with feathers. Typically described as tall, slender, blonde women with pale, glowing skin and fiery eyes, a fairymaid may use her power to "turn" a man's head although more recently this power has been discovered to affect people of all genders.

Fairymaids are phasic in nature and can shift between solid and incorporeal forms at will. This change affects their entire bodies; they cannot become partially incorporeal and partially solid.

Fairymaids have powerful fire-based magical capabilities. They have the power to bring about drought, burn a farmer's crops, or cause cattle to die of high fever. A fairymaid can also change her appearance into a monstrous bird capable of flinging fire at her enemies.

They have a strong affinity for nature and an instinctual knowledge of herb lore. It is possible for a human to learn from them, but almost always at the cost of great time and attention.

Fairymaids' main food source is attention. They can derive nourishment from other creatures noticing and thinking about them. To that end, they cast a sort of hypnotic spell on people that causes them to be fascinated with the fairymaid, providing the fairymaid ample nourishment. They also enjoy the nectar of fresh flowers.

A fairymaid colony reproduces in a very strange manner. During the spring and fall equinoxes and during the summer solstice, a fairymaid colony will start dancing at dusk and continue until sunrise. This dance is captivating to any creature who encounters it and they will join the dance, while the fairymaids feed on the attention and energy, using that energy to produce new children. Fairymaids are adept at hiding their offspring, but it is estimated that they mature at a rate similar to that of human children.

In rare cases a fairymaid and a human male may produce a child in the typical human manner. Any resulting children are exclusively female, and can pass for human children in all ways. They do tend to be captivating in the manner of a fairymaid and have a knack for herb lore. These traits can be passed down the bloodline, but they become weaker with each successive generation.

A juvenile fairymaid is called a child. The collective noun for a group of fairymaids is a colony (a living group) or a crowd (a general group).

HABITAT: Fairymaids live in wooded areas throughout North America. They prefer temperate climates, and become rarer to the deep north and south.

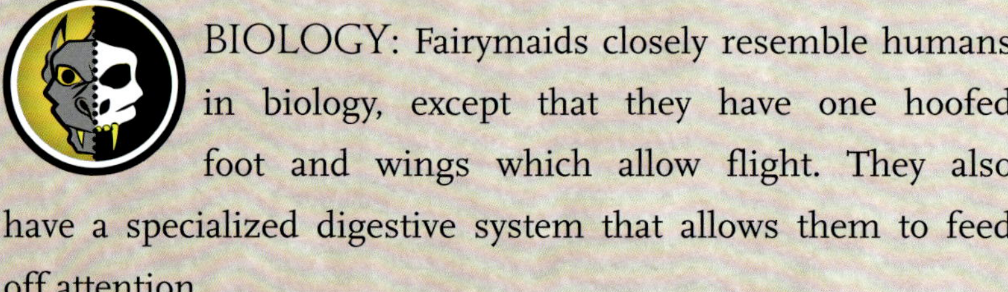

BIOLOGY: Fairymaids closely resemble humans in biology, except that they have one hoofed foot and wings which allow flight. They also have a specialized digestive system that allows them to feed off attention.

DIET: The main diet of a fairymaid is attention, which they cultivate through mesmerism of other creatures, especially human males. They will also consume flower nectar which they consider a special treat. It is believed that they could consume human food, but choose not to for some reason.

MAGICAL USES: Feathers from a fairymaid wing can be used to fashion a cloak which allows flight. They are also used as the cores of wands. It is possible to trade with fairymaid colonies, especially for difficult to find herbs.

Note: Fairymaids are considered a protected species by the North American Council of Five. They are considered sentient beings with intelligence equal to humans. Harvesting a fairymaid for parts carries with it the same penalties as harvesting a human for parts.

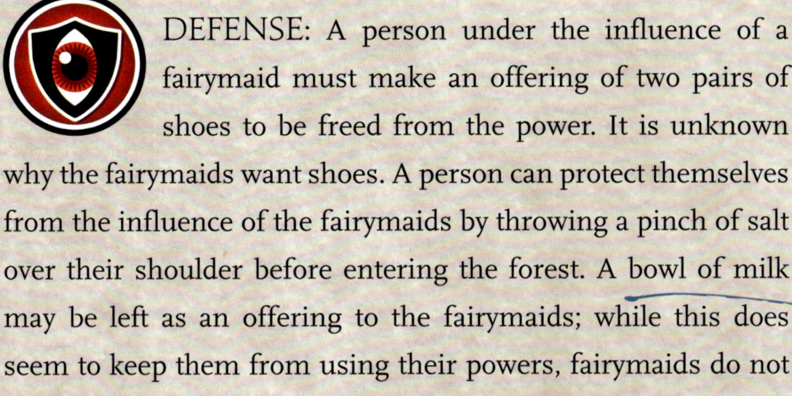

DEFENSE: A person under the influence of a fairymaid must make an offering of two pairs of shoes to be freed from the power. It is unknown why the fairymaids want shoes. A person can protect themselves from the influence of the fairymaids by throwing a pinch of salt over their shoulder before entering the forest. A bowl of milk may be left as an offering to the fairymaids; while this does seem to keep them from using their powers, fairymaids do not drink milk.

A mage with a disciplined mind can willfully divert their attention away from fairymaids while in meditative trances. The resulting polarity reversal will cause the fairymaids to become obsessed with whoever is ignoring them. While this may seem desirable, it is in fact courting disaster as fairymaids are unaccustomed to not getting what they want and the tantrums will escalate to violence. Just give them the damn shoes.

FIDDLE SPIDER

Argiope ascheta lesser and *Argiope ascheta greater*

FAMILY: *Chimerical Insectoid* — which includes arachnids for some reason...
CLASSIFICATION: *Para-sapient*
MANIFESTATION: *Corporeal*
PRONUNCIATION: *FID-dell SPY-dehr*

In 1683, cryptozoologist Arisonda Wellington of Destiny Province attempted to fuse two native creatures, the orb spider and the camel cricket, in order to make a musical spider. She successfully engineered both male and female fiddle spiders but her creations escaped into the wild and multiplied. Now the common lesser fiddle spider is a nuisance pest in almost every Magimundi household in the Americas.

Fiddle spiders are hardy creatures able to thrive in nearly every environment, but they prefer cool, dark places like basements and garages. They are insectivores, using their music to lure unwitting prey to their webs where they may be trapped and devoured.

They have eight legs of which two sets can produce music simultaneously, allowing them to play harmony. Sometimes their music can be hauntingly beautiful and sometimes it can keep a Wizard up all night as the fiddle spider will play its tune as it wishes, night or day.

The adult common lesser fiddle spider grows to about 1 inch in length. It has six jointed legs like a cricket and two front legs like a spider. It has the mouth of a spider with two pincers on either side. It has eight eyes across the top of its head. Luckily, the fiddler spider is not venomous.

In the year 1842, cryptozoologist Regina St. Cartier, also of Destiny Province, experimented with enlarging the fiddle spider and increasing its intelligence with the goal of creating a profitable fiddle spider orchestra. She was successful and her trained spider orchestra was famous for a few years.

But, having learned nothing from her predecessor, she also allowed her creations to escape and now the greater fiddle spider is a common sight in the North American northeast. Like its smaller version, the greater fiddle spider plays music to lure prey to its webs, but it not only preys on insects, it also preys on small rodents like mice and shrews.

The greater fiddle spider is far more intelligent than a common spider. It can be kept as a pet and even taught tricks, especially to play music on command. Several greater fiddle spiders can work together to play well-known tunes. They are also commonly used as familiars in Destiny Province.

The greater fiddle spider can grow to about 5 inches in body length with legs up to 6 inches. It has the same physical characteristics as the lesser spider only proportionally larger. Fiddle spiders are quick and the greater fiddle spider can run in bursts of 3 feet per second, or about 2 miles per hour. They can strike quickly, enveloping their prey in web sacs to be eaten later.

Male fiddle spiders attract mates through a musical mating call. The females lay egg sacs which are dormant throughout the winter and hatch in the springtime. An egg sac can contain over 50 fertile eggs. Greater and lesser fiddle spiders do not cross-breed; greater fiddle spiders will devour lesser fiddle spiders. Lesser fiddle spiders are cannibalistic, but greater fiddle spiders were created to work together and do not view each other as prey.

A juvenile fiddle spider is called a nymph. The nymph stage lasts for one month for a lesser fiddle spider and three months for a greater fiddle spider. The nymph will go through several moltings before it reaches adulthood. A lesser fiddle spider lives for only a few months and dies in the winter. A greater fiddle spider can live up to five years in captivity.

The collective noun for a group of fiddle spiders is an orchestra, or a cacophony.

HABITAT: Lesser fiddle spiders are found all over the Americas. Greater fiddle spiders are native to Destiny Province, although they are quickly moving into the neighboring provinces as well. They are kept as pets and familiars by Magimundi from all the provinces. All fiddle spiders prefer dark, cool habitats.

BIOLOGY: Fiddle spiders are an unholy combination of the camel cricket and the orb spider. The vast majority of their biology is spider-like, but they can rub their legs together to produce music. Greater fiddle spiders have an increased intelligence.

DIET: Lesser fiddle spiders are insectivores. Fully grown greater fiddle spiders will also consume small mammals like mice and shrews.

MAGICAL USES: Greater fiddle spiders can be kept as pets or familiars. Lesser fiddle spiders are considered a nuisance animal; they cannot be used as pest control for they are as likely to eat beneficial insects as harmful ones. The webs of the fiddle spider can be gathered and used in spells and potions but cannot be formed into silk. The legs of the greater fiddle spider are too fragile to be used as wands. Some Wizards have attempted to use them as wand cores, but they are not particularly suited for that either. The molted skin and assorted organs of the greater fiddle spider can be used in spells and potions.

I may or may not be working on a special project to weaponize the fiddle spider's music. Training the greater fiddle spider to relentlessly play screeching or cacophonous music could prove useful in certain situations.

It is believed that the mating song of the greater fiddle spider could be used to create a love spell. Wizards are experimenting with this, but have yet to produce successful results.

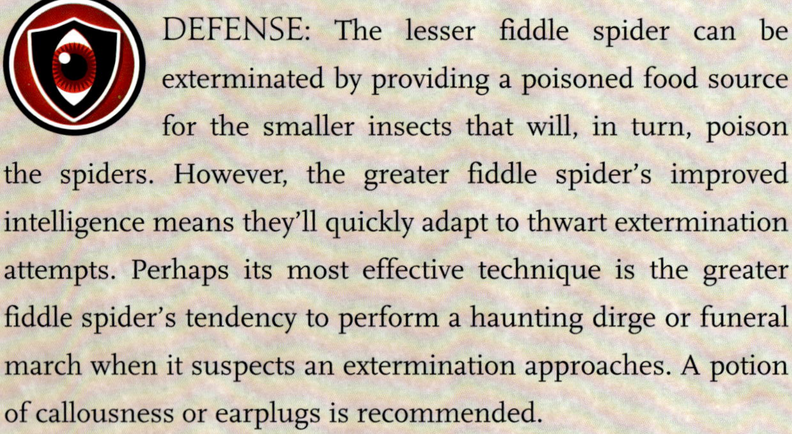

DEFENSE: The lesser fiddle spider can be exterminated by providing a poisoned food source for the smaller insects that will, in turn, poison the spiders. However, the greater fiddle spider's improved intelligence means they'll quickly adapt to thwart extermination attempts. Perhaps its most effective technique is the greater fiddle spider's tendency to perform a haunting dirge or funeral march when it suspects an extermination approaches. A potion of callousness or earplugs is recommended.

Fiji Mermaid

Simian piscus

FAMILY: *Ichthyolios*
CLASSIFICATION: *Non-sapient*
MANIFESTATION: *Corporeal*
PRONUNCIATION: *FĒ-jē/MER-mād*

These stories are a fabrication. I myself have spent considerable time with Fiji mermaids and have not observed any unusual aggressive behavior, and my services (for a fee) are at the ready for anyone who wishes an expert guide to Fiji mermaid domestication.

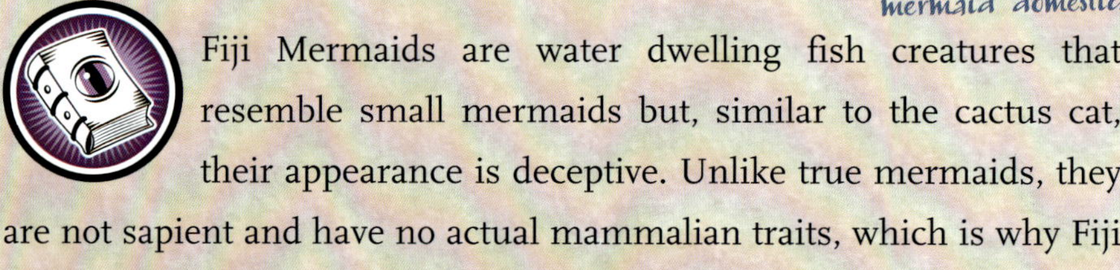

Fiji Mermaids are water dwelling fish creatures that resemble small mermaids but, similar to the cactus cat, their appearance is deceptive. Unlike true mermaids, they are not sapient and have no actual mammalian traits, which is why Fiji mermaids are not considered to be Chimerical.

Adult Fiji mermaids grow to approximately one to two feet long. Fiji mermaids are clever and easily trained, making them popular pets for magi in the South Pacific, where they originate. However, while a juvenile Fiji mermaid is both docile and cute it can become increasingly aggressive, nasty, or brutish as it matures.

European sailors and colonists were "gifted" Fiji mermaids upon arrival to the islands, and they were considered a novelty and a sign of wealth and influence among European and New World mages. Opportunists mounted expeditions to capture and sell Fiji mermaids to magi of means and the numbers proliferated, making them less exclusive and desired once they were more common. In addition, the Fiji mermaids' more aggressive tendencies began to appear. Notable examples include Phineas Gaffney, who, after taking a moonlight swim *au naturale* in the large fountain at his estate, was found in the morning missing various appendages. See also Mercy Montclair (The One-Eared Witch of Mobile), who was attacked by her pet Fiji mermaid while in an epsom salts soak after a long day of wyvern wrangling. As a result of these two trends, Fiji mermaids were largely abandoned in the mid-19th century by families who had bought them as pets for children. These "free" abandoned Fiji mermaids made their way to the shores of the Americas where they flourished. They are now considered an invasive species and are damaging the cryptid ecosystems off the coasts of North and South America.

Fiji mermaids go through three stages of development between birth and adulthood. As larvae they carry with them a yolk-sac which provides nutrition. After developing scales and working limbs they are called handlings, which are typically about the size of an adult human hand. At about 10 months of age, the handling will grow tooth ridges and become an adult. Like fish, Fiji mermaids continue to increase in size as they mature. Fiji mermaids average 3-4 feet in length, though the largest specimen on record was nearly 7 feet long and weighed close to 1,000 pounds. The collective noun for a group of Fiji mermaids is a school.

Fiji mermaid is a local delicacy in the south Pacific, but it has never caught on in the Americas.

HABITAT: Fiji Mermaids are native to the south Pacific but after being released into the wild they have flourished on the east and west coasts of North and South America.

BIOLOGY: Fiji mermaids appear humanoid from the waist up but are entirely fish-like in nature. They breathe through gills and reproduce by laying eggs in the same manner as other fish. Male and female Fiji mermaids are easily obtained. Fiji mermaids are omnivorous, eating both animal and vegetable matter, and have been known to scavenge the leftovers of other animals.

MAGICAL USES: All parts of the Fiji mermaid have magical uses, including the bones, teeth, eyes, cartilage, scales, and eggs. Fiji mermaids can be trained and some magi use them as pets or familiars, although Fiji mermaids cannot survive outside of salt water for more than a few minutes.

DEFENSE: Of particular effectiveness is the fact that the Fiji mermaids are absolutely obsessed with opals. Having a few in a pocket allows for an easy escape for the well-prepared Wizard in addition to some fantastic entertainment, as Fiji mermaids will turn upon each other in savage violence in order to be the one to claim the opal. Visibly wearing opal jewelry in the presence of Fiji mermaids is not recommended.

GHOST HELICOPRION

Helicoprion spectral

FAMILY: Spirit
CLASSIFICATION: Non-sapient
MANIFESTATION: Spectral
PRONUNCIATION: gōst/HE-lē-KOP-rē-on

Helicoprion were a long-lived genus of shark-like fish that prowled the oceans 290-250 million years ago before vanishing in the Early Triassic period. Almost all existing fossil specimens consist of impressions of the unique circular patterns of Helicoprion teeth known as "tooth whorls," similar in pattern to a circular saw.

Ghost helicoprion are the spectral remains of these prehistoric fish. They swim through the air as if underwater. Given where the spirits are found, it is suspected that that the various species of helicoprion lived off the southwestern coast of Gondwana, and later, Pangaea.

Ghost helicoprion do not mate or produce offspring and, like most spirits, they are presumed to be immortal until banished. The collective noun for a group of ghost helicoprion is a shoal. Ghost helicoprion tend to be solitary creatures, though.

Ghost helicoprion are highly dangerous and are not to be approached. Although they are largely non-corporeal, their whorling circular teeth can do a great deal of damage, easily taking off limbs which they are unable to swallow or digest.

They cannot be permanently banished. A particular one that roams near Lake Michigan has a distinctive pattern of scars on its left side, and has returned from what appeared to be successful banishments. This is either a unique property of these ghosts, or the result of some other strange effect. A great deal of interested parties want to understand how a ghost can be made to be resistant to banishing, so research into this creature could be quite lucrative if successful. I may be interested in sponsoring a team, though I'm unfortunately overbooked and could not investigate this creature myself. Not that I'm scared of its lethality! That could not be further from the truth.

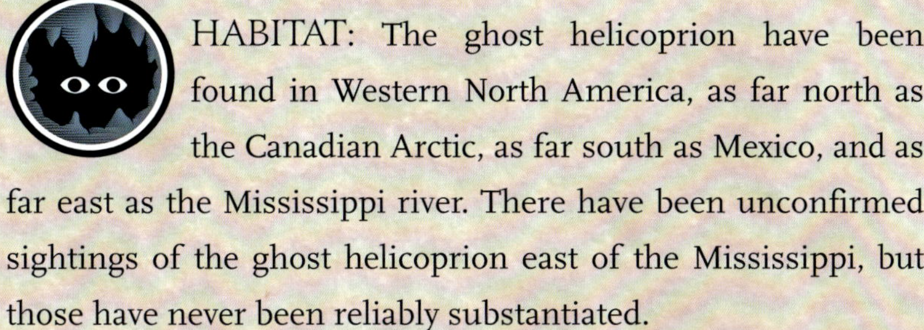

HABITAT: The ghost helicoprion have been found in Western North America, as far north as the Canadian Arctic, as far south as Mexico, and as far east as the Mississippi river. There have been unconfirmed sightings of the ghost helicoprion east of the Mississippi, but those have never been reliably substantiated.

BIOLOGY: Like a typical ghost, helicoprion are entirely spectral. They do not eat, breathe, eliminate, or mate.

MAGICAL USES: There are no magical uses for the ghost helicoprion. They cannot be trained and, being spectral, have no parts which can be harvested for magical uses. A genuine ghost helicoprion tooth would fetch a tidy sum from collectors, but so far only fakes have surfaced.

DEFENSE: Like most ghosts, they can be banished or warded against, but it's quite important to note that the physical properties of their bite can be quite effective in ways that standard ghostly attacks are not. Likewise, they are exceptionally fast and persistent once they have taken notice of potential prey. Spells that cause a blinding flash are particularly effective at disorienting them. They have shown no signs of gaining sentience in their spectral state, so attempts at communication or reason have proven to be entirely ineffective.

GILLYGALOO

Averine quadratum

FAMILY: Averine
SAPIENCE: Non-sapient
MANIFESTATION: Corporeal
PRONUNCIATION: GIL-lē-GAL-lu

The gillygaloo is an unusual bird with a cube-shaped body. It has the other usual characteristics of a bird—a beak, wings, feathers, and so forth—and these are all of normal size and shape.

The gillygaloo nests on the slopes of the Rocky Mountains and has adapted to its surroundings by laying cubic eggs, which are less likely to roll downhill. Gillygaloo eggs are both edible and a useful component in the creation of potions and other magical objects.

An adult gillygaloo can reach about 11 inches in length and can weigh up to 16 pounds. It tends to be brown and grey with yellow legs and short talons. The gillygaloo is another excellent example of where the mundane laws of science fall short, as despite its unique shape and the so-called Laws of Aerodynamics, they have no more difficulty flying than any other bird.

The gillygaloo has a number of unusual vocalizations. It can howl "ooo-weee" during mating season when it is looking for a mate or "nahm-nahm" when it has found food. Its danger call is "ahhhh-ohhhh."

Gillygaloos and their eggs are edible, and some ranchers keep gillygaloo farms as the birds taste like chicken. The ease of storing and transporting gillygaloo carcasses and eggs have made them a staple food source among the Magimundi.

In the wild, a gillygaloo will typically lay about five eggs in the spring. A juvenile gillygaloo takes about five months to mature. They will migrate south along the Rockies in the late fall and back again in the early spring.

A juvenile gillygaloo is called a pip. The collective noun for a group of gillygaloos is a flock.

HABITAT: Gillygaloos make their nests on the slopes of the Rocky Mountains. They migrate south to New Mexico and Kansas in the winter and to Colorado, Idaho, and Utah in the summer.

BIOLOGY: With the exception of their square anatomy, the gillygaloo resembles a smaller version of a wild turkey. Unlike a turkey, they have feathered heads, although their feathers are very much like turkey feathers.

DIET: Gillygaloos are omnivorous. They consume seeds, nuts, berries, and even pine cones. They also eat insects, small reptiles, and amphibians.

MAGICAL USES: Gillygaloos are a popular food source, as are their eggs. Their eggs can also be used in a wide variety of alchemical productions. It is possible to brew some potions inside the gillygaloo eggshell which makes them last six times longer. Their eggs can be hard boiled and magically preserved to be used as dice, which are highly resistant to spells that would influence their results.

Delicious! My first choice of breakfast.

Gillygaloo feathers can be used in spells where numerology is important. They can be enchanted to make a quill that, when used, automatically provides the results for simple arithmetic (Such quills are not allowed at any Primaschola or Magischola in the United States).

The breastbone of the gillygaloo can be broken into four parts at the corners then fused together to make a wand core. Gillygaloos

All experts know that there are countless ways and methods to influence an allegedly random outcome. But as far as dice go, hard-boiled Gillygaloo eggs are one of the best ways to get as near to tamper-proof as possible. I can demonstrate this for a reasonable fee.

have been used as familiars; but they are not very intelligent, so they are considered a familiar of last resort.

DEFENSE: Gillygaloo are not exactly threatening, but due to their increased density, one may stub a toe if they try to kick the bird. There are tales told of abusive humans who come under attack by a flock of gillygalloos seeking vengeance, but this has never been documented.

GOBWIN

(AKA ERFWORLD GOBLIN, ERF GOBLIN)

Twoglodytam balder

FAMILY: *Humanoid*
CLASSIFICATION: *Para-sapient*
MANIFESTATION: *Corporeal*
PRONUNCIATION: *GOB-win*

Gobwins are small (about 3 feet tall, standing erect), horned, bipedal humanoids. Their skin is a uniform green, similar to the darker edge of a slice of ripe avocado. They typically wear simple black coverings resembling togas or loincloths. They have no outward characteristics to distinguish gender, and it is not known if gobwins have distinct sexes (see biology). They are often armed with metal weapons or tools, and are capable melee fighters, even against much larger creatures.

Highly social creatures, Gobwins organize themselves into tribes, which are defined magically and are centered around one or more chiefs. Gobwins are fully sapient, and have their own language, which contains some striking cognates with human language and culture, such as "sudoku," "tamagotchi" and "ikea." A few individuals can speak an uncanny version of English, indistinguishable from a Midwestern American dialect, which they refer to as "Language."

Gobwins are sometimes known as "Erf Goblins" or "Erfworld Goblins," because they have identified their place of origin as "Erfworld." It is not known if this represents a larger subterranean realm, an alien planet, or perhaps even another plane of existence.

There is no such thing a juvenile Gobwin. The collective noun for a small group of Gobwins is a stack.

The tribal structure that Gobwins adopt seems to involve interesting forms of magical telepathy, which they call "Thinkamancy." The chief(s) of the tribe can remotely sense what Gobwin scouts are observing, and also send orders to all members of the tribe, wherever they are. This makes Gobwins extremely difficult to approach, if they do not wish to be, and nearly impossible to surprise.

HABITAT: The known Gobwins of North America are entirely subterranean dwellers, found mostly in Western Montana within Flathead National Forest and Glacier National Park, and more recently in the Canadian Rockies near Banff. They inhabit abandoned (or occasionally active) mines, natural caves, and tunnels of their own making. Given their biomagical need for gems, it should not be surprising that Gobwins are driven to dig. Their primary magical power is to bore through solid rock, eliminating the spoil magically and leaving structurally stable tunnels supported by wooden beams (which they either materialize or transmogrify from the waste rock).

As such, they have become a nuisance to at least two mining operations in Western Montana. A reported attempt to partner with a Gobwin tribe to use their tunneling abilities was rejected on the perplexing grounds that the mining company was not "a side." This apparently meant that the mining company was unable to pay the Gobwins directly in "shmuckers" (see biology).

I have tried to negotiate with these strange creatures, offering gemstones and other valuables. They rebuffed me as well, even going so far as insulting me by calling me a "barbarian." They are clearly delusional creatures.

BIOLOGY: The most unusual aspect of Gobwin nature is their means of sustenance and reproduction, which is entirely magical. They are able to convert gemstones into a form of magical energy (or possibly current, or currency) which they call "shmuckers." This energy is used to materialize (or "pop") either physical items of food, which they then consume normally, or whole new Gobwins which seem to be born into maturity and fully clothed.
When a tribe cannot acquire enough shmuckers to sustain itself

for a given day, some of the Gobwins may dematerialize and be permanently lost ("de-pop").

Gobwins do have internal organs although it is difficult to analyze and understand their use. A dead Gobwin will only last until sunrise and then it -- and all organs harvested from it -- "de-pop" and vanish completely. One other odd note about Gobwins is that, while they do have a circulatory system, they do not bleed when cut.

DIET: Besides their consumption of gems for magical energy, Gobwins can survive on the surface and consume food of various types normal for humanoid species. They have been known to hunt deer and fowl, as well as to gather insects and certain edible plants and fungi. Foraged or hunted food may reduce their need for shmuckers, but probably does not eliminate it entirely.

MAGICAL USES: If you can prove to the Gobwins' satisfaction that you represent a "side," then you can trade with them; they will trade gemstones that they have mined for other gemstones, but find no other trade goods to be of value. Gobwins are not considered a protected species, so it is legal to harvest them for spell components, but there are many Wizards that consider the harvesting of spell components from a para-sapient species to be unethical. Regardless, because components harvested from a Gobwin only last for a short time after the Gobwin "de-pops," they are of limited magical use.

DEFENSE: Gobwins are fierce, but non-magical fighters. They depend on numbers and trickery to overwhelm an opponent. If challenged, they will fall back to a defensible position, almost always in a cave or tunnel.

If engaged in subterranean combat against Gobwins, you should consider the danger of being flanked through solid rock, or of having the ground dug out from beneath you. They may also lay traps to trigger a pit, a fall, or a tunnel collapse against their pursuers. Ambush tactics are also a favorite of Gobwin fighters. Evidence suggests it is also possible that they can employ crude chemical weapons such as chlorine or phosgene gas in t heir traps.

According to all observations, Gobwins seemingly never move at night. In theory, identifying their location before nightfall may allow a successful action against them.

GOLEM

Animus calculus

FAMILY: *Animata*
CLASSIFICATION: *Non-sapient*
MANIFESTATION: *Corporeal*
PRONUNCUATION: *GŌ-ləm*

The earliest accounts of a golem come from the 17th century, when Rabbi Eliyahu of Chelm created the creature from raw clay and used it to perform manual labor. The term golem means "unshaped form," which references Rabbi Eliyahu's supposed utilitarian design. Rabbi Eliyahu's technique for animation, considered by modern experts to be unsurpassed in its performance, has been lost or kept secret.

Today, the definition of "golem" has grown to include any creature corresponding roughly to a humanoid shape or size that is made by animating matter, regardless of the technique or the creature's intended use. Golems are still being produced, but their existence is rare due to the exceptional magical talent required to create one.

Wizards have attempted to create golems in other shapes, but they do not work. There is something about the humanoid shape that is integral to creating a golem. That hasn't kept Wizards from trying, of course. Likewise, golems seem to need to be about the size of a typical adult human. A golem smaller than about 4 feet or taller than 8 feet simply fails to function properly.

Golems are not autonomous or intelligent, but the better-made golems are capable of following such complicated commands that they may give the impression of sapience.

A well-created golem can last a few dozen years before they drain themselves of all magical energy and fall apart. There are rumors of golems that have survived for hundreds, even thousands of years, but there is no evidence to support those rumors. There are rituals which allow Wizards to increase the longevity of a golem; however, they drain the life force of the Wizards who perform them, and they can only be performed by the golem's creators. Because of these difficulties, these spells are rarely used.

Golems are typically created from inorganic material such as sand, clay, or stone; but it is possible to create golems from dead flesh, wood, and liquids. Arch-Mage Thomas Veronicus of Destiny Province claimed to have created an air golem in the year 1799. However, according to his records, the golem quickly dissipated and "blew away." All known attempts to recreate his work have failed.

Golems will always obey the orders of their creators, including obeying the orders of those whom the creators place in charge of them. A golem can be ordered to kill and can even kill its creator; however, golems crumble or dissolve when the life force of their creator is dissipated.

Why is this construct in a cryptozoology textbook? Sure, you could potentially come ~~across one in the wilderness had~~ it been sent or left there, but are these things even properly called creatures?

HABITAT: Golems exist wherever they are created and commanded to go.

Further, golems are not native to the Americas. Why are they included in this cryptozoology textbook?

BIOLOGY: At minimum, golems require a source of magical energy to animate them and an enchantment to direct them. A disruption to either the energy source or to the enchantment will cause the golem to cease functioning.

DIET: The magical energy required to activate a golem is significantly greater than what most magi can produce on their own. There are some exceptionally efficient designs that allow for golems to operate for centuries, but eventually, all golems will deplete their power source and cease functioning.

MAGICAL USES: Beyond their designed use, golems can sometimes surprise their designers with their interpretations of the commands they are given. Golem parts do not make useful components.

Note: It is forbidden by the laws of the Magimundi to create a golem from the bodies of sapient creatures. These so-called "flesh golems" are assaults on the dead, and while not technically necromancy, they are nonetheless prohibited.

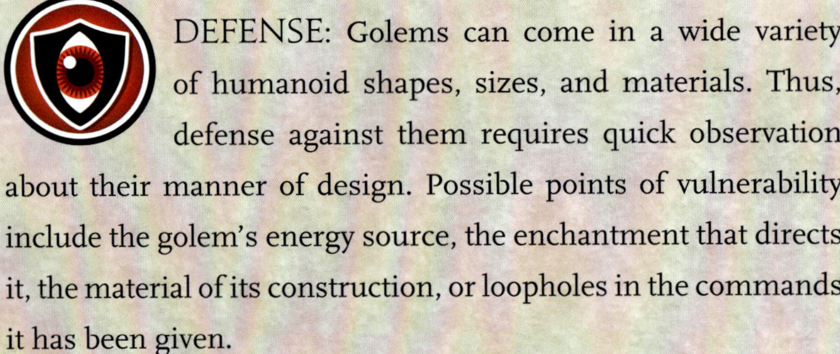

DEFENSE: Golems can come in a wide variety of humanoid shapes, sizes, and materials. Thus, defense against them requires quick observation about their manner of design. Possible points of vulnerability include the golem's energy source, the enchantment that directs it, the material of its construction, or loopholes in the commands it has been given.

GREMLIN

Vexatio dahl

FAMILY: *Humanoid*
CLASSIFICATION: *Semi-sapient*
MANIFESTATION: *Corporeal*
PRONUNCIATION: *GREM-lin*

The gremlin was first discovered in the early 20th century by British magi. Gremlins have an unusual affinity for complexity and technology and will infest any area with significantly high technology, including artifacts that exude magical energies. They range from 3 feet to 5 feet in height, are orangish-tan in color, and are hairless, except for unruly tufts that grow from the head and ears. Gremlins tend to walk upright like chupacabra.

Gremlins are excellent at hiding and evasion. When cornered, they will attack with claws and teeth but only do enough damage to get away. Gremlins like to nest in tangles of wires, often damaging whatever device is on the other end.

A juvenile gremlin is called a grunt. The collective noun for a group of gremlins is an infestation. Gremlins live in small groups from anywhere in the single digits to the mid-forties in number. The largest infestation of gremlins was counted at 108 [See Josiah Wigfall at Redcliffe Plantation and Ezra Blackwolf and the Fumarole Funicular infestation].

Gremlins are clever creatures and have some problem-solving capabilities. They are quite curious and will tend to investigate new surroundings thoroughly.

It is considered bad luck to kill a gremlin. One is supposed to appease the gremlins by leaving them food, hopefully in exchange for them not damaging your equipment. Nonetheless, there do exist gremlin exterminators who rely on a number of charms to ward off the supposed bad luck.

HABITAT: The gremlin can be found in temperate, tropical, and subtropical zones. It is believed that they originally burrowed underground; however, infestations now occur exclusively in man-made buildings or mechanical transportation. It is unknown what draws gremlins to technology, but they seem to have an innate desire to tangle themselves up in ducts and wiring. Chilicothe and the Fumarole Funicular are particularly vulnerable to these creatures.

BIOLOGY: An adult gremlin can grow to up to 5 feet in height. Gremlins can live up to 15 years in the wild. One subspecies of gremlin has flaps of skin connecting its wrists to its torso, similar to the flying squirrel, and may use them to glide short distances.

DIET: Gremlins are omnivorous although they tend toward a carnivorous diet, preferring vermin such as mice and beetles. They also devour snipe.

MAGICAL USES: Gremlin skin, bones, teeth, and eyes are all known potion components. No parts of the gremlin are used to create a wand. Those who try often suffer catastrophic effects.

DEFENSE: The real concern is the bad luck associated with killing a gremlin, which is not to be diminished in significance. With that in mind, non-aggressive techniques of pacification are strongly suggested.

Attempts to appease gremlins with alcohol have backfired disastrously as the gremlins become addicted quickly and demand more. Gremlin exterminators alone know the secret to eliminating these creatures without suffering the consequences. Do not attempt to fight or demonstrate aggression towards a gremlin under any circumstances.

I have, of course, through careful experimentation, discovered the secret to warding against the gremlin's bad luck but have been privately paid a considerable sum of Leeuwendaalders to keep this secret on behalf of a reputable extermination firm. However, this is, as are all things, negotiable.

HOMUNCULUS

Animus carnem

FAMILY: *Animata*
CLASSIFICATION: *Para-sapient*
MANIFESTATION: *Corporeal*
PRONUNCIATION: *ho-MUNK-yu-lus*

A homunculus is created by removing a piece of a Wizard's body and animating the flesh. A homunculus retains a small portion of the Wizard's intelligence and has a telepathic connection to its creator.

Originally intended to be a genuine creation of life—a Wizard parthenogenesis, so to speak—the homunculus was an abject and embarrassing failure in that regard. However, the creature proved to be rather useful, just the same, as certain misanthropic Wizards with no patience for apprentices or verbally explaining instructions found that a homunculus is the perfect lab assistant: It can be given detailed commands with merely a clearly visualized idea of the intended result and a perfunctory grunt.

As part of its creation, the flesh of the Wizard is stitched into a human form. The Wizard must use their own flesh as animating the flesh of others creates a flesh golem instead. Homunculi need not be created in the shape of a human being, but a basic humanoid gives the best results. One could theoretically sever one's hand, stitch the wrist closed, and create a hand-shaped homunculus that walks upon its fingers, although whether this is a desirable outcome depends on the creating Wizard. On more than one occasion, a Wizard has created a homunculus from a tumor or diseased organ that was removed from their body.

There is at least one documented case where a Wizard attempted to create a homunculus from his entire body. The spell misfired, causing the Wizard to first turn into a wrinkled, miniature, gnome-like version

Creepiest thing I ever saw was a homunculus made from a recently removed gall bladder and diseased appendix. Its gall stones made a clinking sound whenever it moved.

of himself, then to turn into a wrinkled, miniature, gnome-like corpse. Since those initial attempts, there are no known accounts of any Wizard attempting to replicate this spell.

Homunculi are rather fragile creatures and, in their eagerness to please their creators, have an unfortunate tendency to perish rather frequently (and often hilariously) in accidents.

HABITAT: Homunculi exist wherever they are created, never straying far from their Wizard.

BIOLOGY: Homunculi are usually less than 10 inches tall. They can have hair if the flesh that was used had hair. They can be created with voice and a means to speak, but they usually echo their Wizard in a high-pitched voice, which some find to be profoundly annoying. On average they will live about three weeks, though some have survived as long as six months with attentive care. They expire dramatically, flailing about in their final moments before shriveling up into a pile of dusty, dried flesh.

or profoundly hilarious.

DIET: Homunculi survive by means of their magical connection to their creator and do not eat, drink, or excrete. They can, however, sense when their Wizard is hungry or thirsty and will attempt to bring them food.

The most common cause of homunculi death: accidentally boiling themselves while trying to prepare a cup of tea.

MAGICAL USES: Expired homunculi still retain a connection to their creator, and that connection can be exploited in the usual ways. It's strongly recommended that expired homunculi be properly disposed of. You can make your own homunculus your familiar, but this is ill-advised.

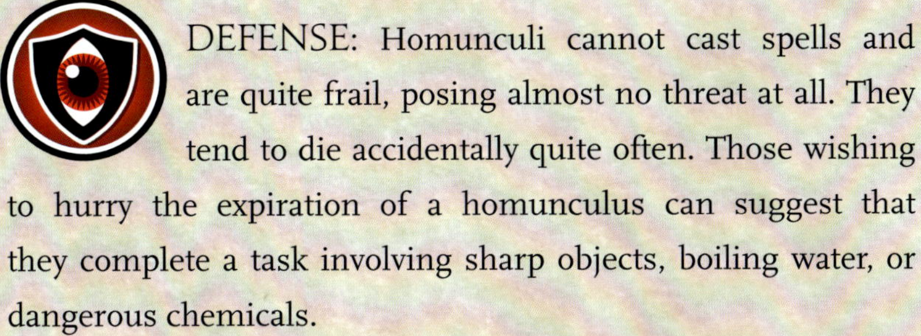

DEFENSE: Homunculi cannot cast spells and are quite frail, posing almost no threat at all. They tend to die accidentally quite often. Those wishing to hurry the expiration of a homunculus can suggest that they complete a task involving sharp objects, boiling water, or dangerous chemicals.

HOOP SNAKE

Agkistrodon circulus

FAMILY: *Reptilian*
CLASSIFICATION: *Non-sapient*
MANIFESTATION: *Corporeal*
PRONUNCIATION: *HŪP/snāk*

The hoop snake is closely related to the common American pit vipers such as the cottonmouth and copperheads and, like their cousins, produce a potent, toxic venom. A human bitten by a hoop snake experiences symptoms such as severe pain, swelling, weakness, difficulty breathing, hemorrhaging, gangrene, fever, vomiting, and in rare instances, death.

Normally, a hoop snake slithers like other snakes. However, when hunting, it latches onto its own tail and rolls toward its intended prey at speeds reaching up to 40 miles per hour in short bursts. When the hoop snake reaches its prey, it will strike with its mouth or tail as both have venom sacs.

Hoop snakes are reticulated and tend to be colored so that they blend into the landscape. A mature hoop snake can reach 8 feet in length, which allows them to form a hoop of about 2 and a half feet in diameter.

Like other snakes, hoop snakes are ovoviviparous, producing eggs that remain in the mother until they hatch. A mother hoop snake in the final stages of holding a brood may refuse to hoop for fear of damaging the eggs. Hoop snakes reproduce as a hoop with the male latching on to the tail of the female and vice versa. The resulting hoop will roll in circles until the mating is concluded.

A newly hatched hoop snake is called a hatchling. A juvenile hoop snake is called a neonate. The collective noun for a group of hoop snakes is a pit.

HABITAT: The hoop snake can be found throughout the Americas. They prefer large open areas, such as prairies, that make rolling easy.

BIOLOGY: Hoop snakes are similar to pit vipers with the exception of the stinger with venom sacs on their tails.

DIET: Hoop snakes are carnivorous, preferring small mammals as prey. Fully-grown hoop snakes need to feed about once a month.

MAGICAL USES: The venom of the hoop snake can be used in many potions and charms and is used for producing its anti-venom. The stinger of the hoop snake can be attached to a wand to empower offensive spells. Hoop snakes can be enchanted to be used as familiars. The bones, scales, and eyes of the hoop snake can be used for assorted potions and charms. Three linked hoop snakes forming interlocking rings can be used for divination.

This can only be done while the wand is originally being fashioned, not after the fact. Do not waste your money on the hoop snake stinger wand-extenders some charlatans attempt to sell. I regret my previous endorsement.

DEFENSE: A human cannot outrun a hoop snake. The most effective defense against hoop snakes is to hide behind a large object, which the hoop snake will invariably strike, or to climb a tree or over a fence. If bitten by a hoop snake, go to the nearest magical healer who can provide an antivenom. Mundane hospitals can also provide antivenoms in an emergency; just say that you were bitten by a copperhead.

Hoop snakes rely on forward momentum to roll, so running uphill ~~can be quite effective as a means of escape.~~ Veteran handlers, like myself, can swat the hoop snake from the side safely while striking the non-pointy-and-venomous ends.

HUMFAERIE

Homo pinnatus vegrandis

FAMILY: *Humanoid*
CLASSIFICATION: *Para-sapient*
MANIFESTATION: *Corporeal*
PRONUNCIATION: *HUM-FĀR-ē*

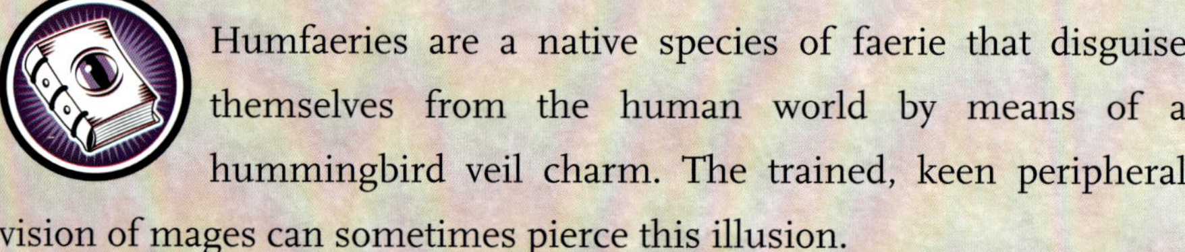

Humfaeries are a native species of faerie that disguise themselves from the human world by means of a hummingbird veil charm. The trained, keen peripheral vision of mages can sometimes pierce this illusion.

Humfaeries were discovered in the early 1800s by the mage farmer Wren Winchester near Sault Ste. Marie, Michigan. Here is the story in her own words:

> *The first time I encountered what I now know was a humfaerie, I was tossing kernels of corn out to the turkeys in my backyard. I heard a strange buzzing noise and looked about, only to discover a ruby throated hummingbird hovering nearby. I didn't think much of it, but decided I would set out a little bowl of sugar water for him. Standing next to the well, I lowered my bucket down into its depths. It hit the surface with a splash. As I began hauling it back up, I happened to catch a glimpse of the hummingbird out of the corner of my eye. To my surprise, it was no bird. It was a tiny person with wings. The expression on my face must have given me away. Once I discovered his true identity, the little faerie man looked just as surprised as I did and quickly disappeared into the woods.*

These faeries earned their name due to the distinctive humming noise they make while in flight, which is especially noticeable when they hover in place. In their natural form, the humfaeries are thin, yet muscular humanoid figures with wings resembling that of a cicada.

Adults range from 3 to 4 inches in height. Though their colorations vary, the majority of these faeries are golden skinned with straight dark hair and brown eyes.

Humfaeries who live east of the Mississippi River prefer to mimic the ruby-throated hummingbird, while those west of the Mississippi tend to resemble black-chinned hummingbirds. To be clear, this is a magical disguise and not an actual transformation. True mages can occasionally see through this disguise if they happen to catch the humfaerie out of the corner of their eyes.

Humfaeries are intelligent and resourceful. They fashion their own weapons and food preparation tools from various woods and stones. They are also known to manufacture their own clothes. Their garments are are woven from spider silk and dyed with readily available flora such as bloodroot, sumac, and yarrow. The curling vines of Concord grapes are used to make jewelry, and for special occasions such as joining ceremonies, humfaeries will wear heirloom pieces carved from mother of pearl or turquoise.

Humfaeries never hunt for sport. They only pursue large insects and juvenile rodents for food. After each kill, they honor the lives of the creatures they take. They favor magic-laced bows and arrows. They can also cast spells for hunting, defense, and everyday use. Rather than wands, humfaeries use crystal shards to help focus their power.

Humfaeries farm spiders for silk. Their homes are often surrounded by a plethora of webs. This serves several purposes. First, they do not have to travel far to bring in their harvest. Second, humans tend to avoid areas littered with webs, so it deters them from venturing too close. On the rare occasion an intruder does approach their territory, the spiders trigger a silent alarm that warns the faeries of potential danger. The humfaeries also tame hornets and yellow jackets, encouraging them to build their nests within the borders of their lands. These trained hives serve as guardians and the first line of defense.

Humfaeries grow crops of mushrooms inside their tree trunks for food, medicine, and other uses. They have been known to trade their farmed mushrooms with humans.

Culturally, these beings are proud, strong, intuitive, and empathic individuals. They communicate in their own language, Faerish, which is taught in many Primaschola and Magischola across the country. Some Humfaeries have learned English, French, Spanish, and other languages to facilitate their trade with humans.

Humfaeries have their own religion, focusing on natural cycles of the moon and seasons and the spirits of plants and animals. They believe in a spirit world and an afterlife, and they have elaborate ceremonies on the solstices and equinoxes.

Humfaeries are social beings with their own organizational mechanisms. They mate for life and have a formalized joining ceremony similar to a human hand fastening. Like humans, humfaeries live in family units. Homes are built by hand out of a thick grayish clay that they excavate from nearby rivers or lakes. Building a new home is the very first thing a newly-joined couple will do after their ceremony. They carve intricate designs into the walls and archways expanding the dwelling as the family expands. The young look after the old who are respected and revered. Life expectancy is around 150 years of age.

Humfaerie homes tend to be part of larger communities housed in inconspicuous, yet enchanted hollowed-out trees. The magic they weave into their homes allows many of them to fit in a single trunk. The clans call these communities kingdoms, and you can find thousands of humfaerie homes in a single trunk.

Humfaerie kingdoms are led by a joined couple referred to as the Queen and King. Each clan kingdom has a ruling couple. Rule is ancestral, passing down through children and relatives as the ruling couple passes. They have week-long coronation ceremonies when crowning a new Queen and King. Each kingdom is ruled according to the laws set by their own ruling couple. Although they prefer peace—and it has not happened in over 150 years as of writing this—the different kingdoms of humfaeries have been known to go to war.

Well, foxfire, times change. It is well-known that there are two humfaerie kingdoms just across the border from each other: one in Mishipeshu Province and one in Thunderbird. They have been hunting on the same lands for about 12 years now and have had some border skirmishes. I would not be surprised if formal war is declared by the end of the first quarter of the 21st century.

While the origin of humfaeries is not completely clear, there is some speculation as to the truth of a story that has been passed down for generations across the Midwest. The legends tells us that many centuries ago, there was a small human village just off the coast of the Great Lakes. It had been an extraordinarily stormy summer, and the crops were stricken with rot. Winter was fast approaching, the food stores were empty, and the villagers were going to starve. Unable to find nourishment, they consulted their ancestral spirits for advice. The spirits guided them to one of their own, whom they had long considered an outcast, and they begged him to save their lives. The solution they received was a curious one. Unbeknownst to them, the outcast was a Wizard. He revealed his wand and cast a spell over all the villagers, transforming them into their current shape, and instilling in them some form of residual magic. The magic humfaeries possess is insufficient to cast spells, so they must use crystals to focus their energies and bodies of water to channel it.

Wendigos deprived of human flesh have been known to gorge themselves on humfaeries, suggesting that the above described origin myth may have a note of truth to it. Humfaeries deny this creation story and claim that they moved to Earth from a spirit realm.

A female juvenile humfaerie is called a hem and a male a haw. The plural of these is hems and haws. The collective noun for a group of humfaeries is a hamper.

HABITAT: There are different clans of humfaeries living in various locations across North America. They tend to congregate near fresh water as it acts as a conduit to amplify their magic. Because of the Great Lakes that surround it, Michigan is a natural home to one of the largest kingdoms of humfaeries in North America. Their individual family homes are made from clay they excavate from the beds of rivers and lakes. They build their kingdoms inside innocuous-looking hollowed out tree trunks.

BIOLOGY: Internally, humfaeries resemble very small human beings. They have insect-like wings.

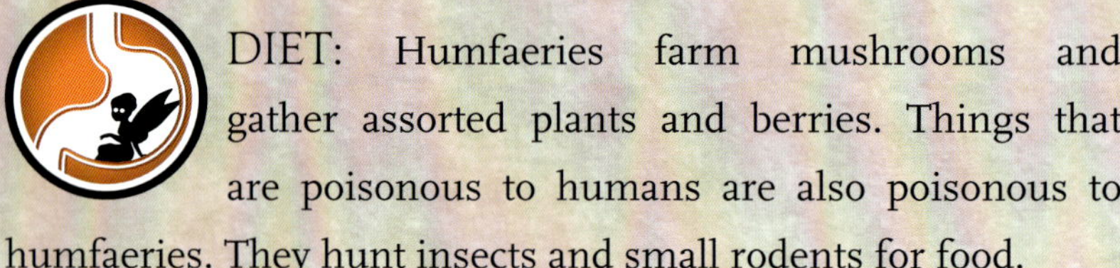

DIET: Humfaeries farm mushrooms and gather assorted plants and berries. Things that are poisonous to humans are also poisonous to humfaeries. They hunt insects and small rodents for food.

MAGICAL USES: Humfaeries have been known to trade with humans. They produce excellent silk cloth and farm rare mushrooms suitable for a variety of purposes. As for the humfaeries themselves, the only body parts of theirs with any magical use whatsoever are their hair and wings. Hair is used for wand cores, while their wings have various uses in spells and charms. The more human parts have little to no magic in them and are useless to wizards. Humfaeries can be made into familiars if they are willing. Such a binding agreement is undertaken at great risk to the humfaerie and Wizard alike, as the humfaerie is banished from its kingdom, and the associated Wizard is likewise shunned and ostracized by humfaerie society.

Note: Humfaeries are considered a protected species by the North American Council of Five. They are considered sentient beings with intelligence equal to humans. Harvesting a humfaerie for parts carries with it the same penalties as harvesting a human for parts.

DEFENSE: Humfaeries favor peace over war, but make no mistake, they are fierce warriors when aggressive action is required. To defend yourself, there are two options:

Firstly, you can create a shield of blinding sunlight. The humfaerie has sensitive eyes, and this temporary blindness typically lasts upwards of a minute, triggering an instinctive flight response. If you have really managed to rile up the wrong clan, employing this tactic will grant you approximately 60 seconds to escape.

Secondly, you can summon a temporary swarm of praying mantises. Mantises are a natural predator of hummingbirds and will eat them in the wild. This option should only be enacted when you have no other way to resolve conflict with the humfaeries. They will disappear, and you will likely never encounter them again.

HUGAG

Rythmopes inarticulatus

FAMILY: *Mammalian*
CLASSIFICATION: *Non-sapient*
MANIFESTATION: *Corporeal*
PRONUNCIATION: *HU-gag*

The hugag is a huge animal of the Lake States. Its range includes the northern area of Mishipeshu Province. In size, the hugag is comparable to the moose which it somewhat resembles. Noticeable differences include its jointless legs, which compel the animal to remain on its feet, and an upper lip so long that attempting to graze results only in trampling it into the dirt.

The head and neck of the hugag are leathery and hairless. Its strangely corrugated ears flop downward and its four-toed feet, long bushy tail, and shaggy coat give the beast an unmistakably prehistoric appearance.

When fully grown, a hugag stands about 13 feet high and weighs around six hundred pounds. The legs of a hugag lack knee, fetlock, or hock joints, so the hugag can't lie down and must sleep standing up. Usually, a hugag braces its splayed feet and leans against a tree to take a nap, and such sleep-trees are often badly and permanently bent.

The hugag never stays in one place for long, and the few magi who have attempted to trail it have failed to find the beast and, in some cases, failed to come back to camp. The hugag has incredible stamina and can travel all day, browsing on twigs, flopping its lip around trees, and stripping bark as occasion offers. At night, it leans against a tree and braces its legs to sleep. A steady diet of pine knots can make a hugag ooze sap from its pores.

The most successful hugag hunters have adopted the practice of notching potential sleep-trees so that they are unstable enough to come down when a hugag leans against them. Trapped under the fallen tree, the hugag is easily dispatched.

The hugag is a gentle animal that does little harm, save when he leans against buildings. Flimsy structures and campsites are often ruined when a hugag decides to take a rest by leaning on one.

A juvenile hugag is called a calf. The collective noun for a group of hugags is a herd.

HABITAT: The hugag lives in central North America, primarily around the Great Lakes region and parts north. They require woodlands to live as they cannot graze or lie down.

BIOLOGY: Hugags most closely resemble moose, although without antlers and with a gentler disposition.

DIET: Hugags are herbivorous and their diet consists mostly of tree bark, leaves, berries, and twigs. They are very fond of pine knots and will gorge on them until they extrude sap from their pores.

MAGICAL USES: Hugags cannot be domesticated, although some magi have successfully managed to use them for transport or as a food source. They make poor familiars. Their pelt can be fashioned into damage resistant leather armor. Their bones can be made into wands, and their teeth can be fashioned into necklaces that can provide extra magical power. Sap exuded by a hugag (commonly known as Hugag Juice) may be harvested and is useful in many herbal concoctions.

Not all that damage resistant. My excessively long hunt, and the jerkin I acquired as a result, could hardly be considered worth it. I broke several ribs testing it!

DEFENSE: Hugags are not aggressive, but their incredible size makes it dangerous to be in their vicinity if they become alarmed. Merely putting some distance between yourself and the Hugag will put you out of danger.

JACKALOPE

Lepus antilocapra

FAMILY: *Mammalian*
CLASSIFICATION: *Non-sapient*
MANIFESTATION: *Corporeal*
PRONUNCIATION: *JAK-A-lōp*

The jackalope is a well-known fearsome critter described as a jackrabbit with antelope horns. The word "jackalope" is a portmanteau of "jackrabbit" and "antelope," although the jackrabbit is not a rabbit and the American antelope is not an antelope.

Only male jackalopes have antlers, but the female jackalope still differs from other hares in that they are faster and appear to have some ability to camouflage themselves. Jackalopes are also highly resistant to magic, making them difficult to manage as familiars or pets.

Normally a shy animal, the jackalope's behavior changes drastically during its mating season in the spring when male jackalopes will lock antlers or attempt to chase other males away in order to secure their access to breeding females.

Hunting jackalopes is extremely dangerous, and anyone attempting it is advised to wear stove-pipe coverings on their legs to protect themselves from being gored. Should you wish to entice a jackalope closer, the best lure by far is whiskey, the jackalope's beverage of choice.

The jackalope can imitate the human voice. During the days of the Old West, when cowboys gathered by the campfires singing at night, jackalopes could be heard mimicking their voices or singing along, usually as a tenor.

A juvenile jackalope is called a leveret. The collective noun for a group of jackalopes is a drove.

HABITAT: The jackalope lives in northwestern North America, primarily around Wyoming. They prefer flat, empty grasslands. Jackalopes are solitary, like hares, and live in simple nests above the ground.

BIOLOGY: Jackalopes are physically hares in their biology except for the growth of antlers. They are preternaturally fast, naturally resistant to magic, and slightly more aggressive than normal hares. Jackalopes have some natural camouflage abilities, as well, and can change the color of their fur to almost any color at will. It is thought that the color reflects their emotional state, but they may also change color just to be difficult.

While, yes, typically antlered creatures shed their antlers and the Jackalopes do not, and therefore they should properly be called horns by a certain strict definition of the terms, the Jackalope's antlers look like antlers so they are called antlers and that's final.

DIET: Jackalopes are herbivorous and their diet consists mostly of leaves, grasses, and assorted fruit and vegetables.

MAGICAL USES: Jackalope pelts can be sewn into boots of speed. Their antlers can be fashioned into puissant wands. Their organs can be used for charms and potions. Their entrails can be read for divination. Jackalope feet can be fashioned into luck charms.

DEFENSE: The stovepipe defense against jackalopes is not unreasonable. Jackalopes have an uncanny ability to be where you least expect them, and even the most experienced hunter can be caught off guard

Quite true for once. Jackalope hunting ~~appears to be about luck, accidents, and having other people take the damage for you.~~ The creatures just don't move according to your expectations.

by the vexing nature of their speed and attack and get seriously injured. The best defense against an aggressive jackalope is a simple levitation spell. Even a leaping attack from a Jackalope isn't nearly as bad as the damage it can inflict with its gore, and most won't even attempt to attack a creature that isn't on the ground.

This is actually the best method of claiming an antler for a wand. Bring some poor chump on the hunt, and when he's been gored, claim the snapped off antler for yourself while tending to his wound.

JERSEY DEVIL

Draco minor igneus New Jersey

FAMILY: *Reptilian*
CLASSIFICATION: *Para-sapient*
MANIFESTATION: *Corporeal*
PRONUNCIATION: *JER-zē/DE-vil*

The Jersey Devil is a legendary creature said to inhabit the Pine Barrens of Southern New Jersey. The Jersey Devil is a kangaroo-like creature with the head of a goat, leathery bat-like wings, horns, small arms with clawed hands, cloven hooves, and a forked tail. It has been reported to move quickly and often is described as emitting a blood-curdling scream.

The Lenape tribes called the area where the Devil is found "Popuessing" meaning "place of the dragon." The Swedish explorers later named it "Drake Kill" ("drake" being a word for dragon, and "kill" meaning channel or arm of the sea (river, stream, etc. in Dutch).

The Jersey Devil is, in fact, a drake: a small dragon. It is centuries old and seems to be the only member of its species. It is speculated that there used to be a race of dragons native to the Americas, all of which went extinct some time ago, except for the Jersey Devil. However, no evidence has been brought forward to confirm this theory. It is still considered a cryptozoological fact that there are no species of dragon native to the Americas.

The Jersey Devil is quite intelligent and magi can, and have, communicated with it. However, as its motives are unknown and it is quick to anger (and quite deadly), the number of people who have survived a conversation with the Jersey Devil is fewer than 15.

The Jersey Devil is capable of flight and has great skill at moving unseen through the tree-tops. It can see in perfect darkness, although using this power causes its eyes to glow red. The scream of the Jersey

Devil can cause bleeding from the ears and eyes, rupturing of the eardrums, and, in some cases, permanent deafness. The Jersey Devil can also breathe flame, although it seems to be rarely willing to do so.

HABITAT: The Jersey Devil lives in a small cave in the Pine Barrens of Southern New Jersey. It has enchanted the cave so that Mundanes cannot find it.

BIOLOGY: The exact biology of the Jersey Devil is unknown, but it is presumed to have a biology similar to the drakes of Europe and Asia.

DIET: The Jersey Devil is omnivorous but subsists mostly on livestock and pets.

MAGICAL USES: The Jersey Devil is magical in nature, and it is presumed that uses for its organs and body-parts would be the same as those of its European cousins.

DEFENSE: Do not taunt the Jersey Devil. Do not compliment the Jersey Devil. Do not laugh in the presence of the Jersey Devil. Do not fart in the presence of the Jersey Devil. If you are carrying food, give every last bit of what you have to the Jersey Devil if it asks, holding nothing back. If the Jersey Devil demands food that you do not have, immediately offer to bring it what it wants. Do not break this promise to the Jersey Devil, but rather than returning directly with the promised items, simply leave the package where it can be found. At all times, remember that your goal is to escape the Jersey Devil alive.

I have been asked by Magisters of Destiny Province to not interact with the Jersey Devil, and therefore, I have no means of confirming any of this. My appeal is pending.

JIWA SETAN

Tenebris umbraculum

FAMILY: *Spirit*
CLASSIFICATION: *Non-sapient*
MANIFESTATION: *Spectral*
PRONUNCIATION: *JĒ-wa/sē-TAHN*

A jiwa setan is a spiritual being that manifests as a dark shadow, and like a shadow, it is two-dimensional. It only hunts during the twilight hours of dusk and dawn when the shadows are the longest. It lies quiescent the rest of the day, sleeping in the shadows of trees or buildings, and moving as the sun moves. Its main food source is strong positive emotion, such as joy or love. A jiwa setan prefers the joy of magic users, but will feast upon the mundanes if necessary.

The victim on which a jiwa setan feeds experiences anhedonia (total lack of pleasure or happiness) for a period of 12 hours (until the following dusk or dawn), but recurring feedings can render this a permanent condition. Victims of the jiwa setan often appear pale and somewhat listless, in addition to their compromised emotional state.

Jiwa setan tend to live solitary lives. They do not age, but they can die from starvation. They avoid bright lights, as they can be damaged or even destroyed by them. Jiwa setan reproduce asexually, by binary fission; when a jiwa setan has grown too large to comfortably fit in the shadows, it will split into two creatures. This happens rarely, perhaps once every few decades.

There are no juvenile jiwa setan. The collective noun for a group of jiwa setan is a nightmare.

HABITAT: Jiwa setan live in the shadows of the Solaris Province, as well as on the islands of the Caribbean Sea. They prefer areas that are naturally shady, but need to be close to humankind to feed.

BIOLOGY: It is difficult to accurately measure the size of a jiwa setan. They seem to be composed entirely of shadow, possess a shadow's flexibility, and are flat to the point of two dimensionality.

DIET: Jiwa setan feed on positive emotions, preferably strong ones from magi, but they will feed on mundanes if necessary.

(Let the buyer beware, the current market appears to be saturated with counterfeit rituals to this end.)

MAGICAL USES: There are rituals that allow magic users to control a jiwa setan, allowing its master to use it as a spy or even an assassin. Part of these rituals involve regular feeding of the jiwa setan on its master; careful balance must be taken so the master does not find themselves lost to their spiraling negative emotions.

DEFENSE: As noted, the jiwa setan is vulnerable to bright lights, and spells that create this effect. Absolute darkness will also drive away the creature, should circumstances mean that extinguishing light sources is far easier than creating them. Recurrent victims of the jiwa setan are very likely in a state of dehydration, having lost all motivation for self-preservation, so rehydration is the first priority of care.

This notion is preposterous. Problems do not go away by merely shutting one's eyes to the presence of a hostile magical creature. No rational explorer or adventurer would even consider this technique.

KUMCHARANGI

Serpens Pinnatus

FAMILY: *Reptilian*
CLASSIFICATION: *Non-sapient*
MANIFESTATION: *Corporeal*
PRONUNCIATION: *kum-char-ĀN-jē*

The Kumcharangi are subterranean winged snakes with a venomous bite. They are highly aggressive and very dangerous. A juvenile Kumcharangi averages about a foot in length, with adults capable of growing as large as ten feet. Their coloring is typically mottled black and brown, and they possess glowing yellow eyes with a nictitating membrane that allow them to see in the dark.

Kumcharangi live underground in burrows and are capable of moving through the soil with great dexterity. They track their prey by the vibrations from above, and attack by bursting from the earth and swallowing the prey whole, if possible.

The wings of a Kumcharangi are black, leathery and extremely flexible, capable of folding flat along their bodies so that they prove no impediment to movement above or below ground. They are used in short gliding flights, or, in unusual cases, dropping from tall trees. The Kumcharangi typically attacks by bursting from the ground and using their wings to glide toward their victim with a distinctive high-pitched scream. Human victims of Kumcharangi have described feelings of paralysis during the attack, although it is uncertain whether this is an unknown secondary characteristic of the scream or simply a normal reaction to seeing a giant winged snake with glowing yellow eyes burst from the soil.

The bite of a Kumcharangi is highly dangerous. An estimated 45% of bite victims will develop *Aphotic Bane,* a disease that gradually robs wizards of their sanity and ultimately requires their permanent hospitalization. Aphotic Bane has a special property that allows it to remain dormant in its host, and there are recorded cases of victims being entirely unaware that they have the Bane until the symptoms manifest years later. Although the ministrations of a Master Healer may slow the progression of the disease, there is currently no cure for Aphotic Bane, and an unknown element in Kumcharangi venom precludes the creation of an antidote.

Kumcharangis tend to live solitary lives, coming together only to mate. A female Kumcharangi will lay up to ten eggs in a clutch, staying to protect the nest until the eggs hatch. Kumcharangis do not develop their venom until they reach adulthood, making juvenile Kumcharangis very vulnerable to predators and poachers. Kumcharangis do not breed well in captivity so they have to be caught in the wild.

A newly hatched Kumcharangi is called a hatchling. A juvenile Kumcharangi is called a neonate. It takes two years for a Kumcharangi to reach adulthood. The collective noun for a group of Kumcharangi is a pit.

HABITAT: The Kumcharangis live in small burrows in the loamy soil of the American southeast. They dislike cold weather and will become sluggish and some even hibernate in the winter months.

BIOLOGY: An adult Kumcharangi can grow to ten feet in length. They can have a wingspan of up to six feet. The glowing eyes are caused by a magical effect; no evidence of bioluminescence have been found. A Kumcharangi will shed its skin about once a month, more often as it grows from neonate to adult.

DIET: The Kumcharangis are carnivorous and will eat small to medium sized mammals. The favored preys of the juvenile are mice and rats. Adult Kumcharangis can eat animals as large as juvenile sheep or goats. A Kumcharangi usually feeds about once a month.

MAGICAL USES: Shed Kumcharangi skin has no magical purpose although it is decorative; fresh skin can be fashioned into charms and gris-gris. Their eyes can be used to make a potion that allows one to see in the dark. Their bones can be used as wands. Other parts of the Kumcharangis can be used for potions, charms, and talismans. Kumcharangi venom loses its toxicity soon after extraction and is not useful as a poison or potion ingredient. Some mages keep Kumcharangis as pets or familiars. They may be devenomed in that case. Kumcharangi can also be trained as guards as long as

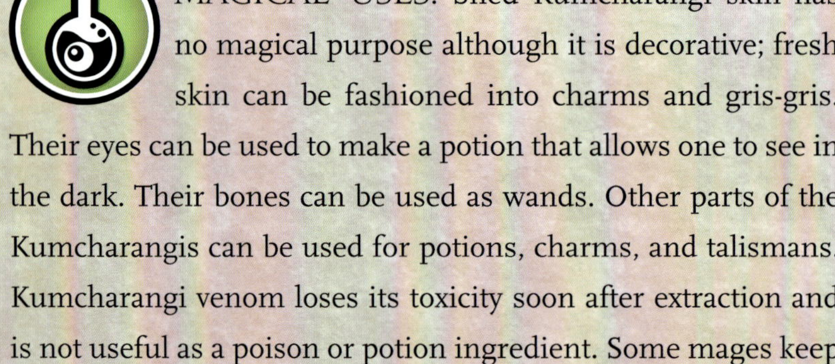

the training starts when they are still hatchlings or neonates. Seeing an albino Kumcharangi is considered a powerful omen that can be positive or negative depending on circumstance.

DEFENSE: Kumcharangi are overall exceptionally resistant to damage with the exception of fire. Among the counter-attacks, only a powerful fire spell can deter a Kumcharangi from completing a gliding charge. Unfortunately, a poorly aimed spell cast in panic has more than once caused a conflagration that saved the Wizard from a venomous bite only to leave a burnt up corpse. Weak or middling fire spells will not have enough oomph to effectively combat a Kumcharangi. Since there is no anti-venom, those unlucky enough to be bitten by a Kumcharangi may be advised to amputate the affected limb to prevent subsequent infection with Aphotic Bane.

It's clear the the author has failed to account for the versatility of heat spells apart from that of fire creation when describing the defense to the Kumcharangi, as it has been documented that a direct heat spell in a Kumcharangi's open mouth during its signature wailing will consistently cause the creature to abort its attack and flee. Likewise it's also been shown that the glide attack of the Kumcharangi can be disrupted by spells that create a strong gust of wind; if it cannot approach you, it cannot bite you.

Of the three documented cases of an emergency field amputation after a Kumcharangi bite to prevent Aphotic Bane, none have ever succeeded in preventing the spread of infection, and may in fact have made things worse with the blood loss negatively impacting the body's resistance to the venom. But hey, go ahead and try it if you're feeling lucky.

LIGHTNING SNAKE

Electrophorus electricus giganticus

FAMILY: *Icthyolios*
CLASSIFICATION: *Non-sapient*
MANIFESTATION: *Corporeal*
PRONUNCIATION: *LĪT-ning/snāk*

The lightning snake is a giant sea creature that generates electricity. Technically, the lightning snake is a giant electric eel, but if we insist on being pedantic then it must be acknowledged that electric eels aren't really eels either, but knifefish, and then we would have to call it the giant lightning knifefish.

An adult lightning snake can reach up to fifty feet in length, and weigh up to 1800 pounds. It is native to the north Pacific Ocean, preferring the coastal waters of the Thunderbird Province. The lightning snake can control the amperage and voltage of its discharge, and can produce bursts up to 25,000 volts. A lightning snake can produce bolts of electricity to stun or even kill its prey. It also uses the lightning for defense and communication.

The higher the voltage and amperage, the shorter the duration of the electrical burst. An adult lightning snake can reliably produce enough energy, for a long enough time, to kill a human being.

The lightning snake is capable of creating thunderstorms at sea, and drawing lightning down from the sky, which it may use to recharge itself when low on power; however, there must be at least minimal cloud cover for the snake to take advantage of this ability.

Lightning snakes have been known to attack sailing ships; however, this is rare. It usually occurs when the ship is transporting cargo the lightning snake finds interesting, although at least one ship has been destroyed by a lightning snake with cryptozoologists aboard attempting to discover more about this elusive creature. This may be correlation, and not causation, but cryptozoologists since have chosen to study other less-deadly creatures.

Lightning snakes are immune to any electrical damage, but they have an odd vulnerability: they can be entirely controlled by a thunderbird. It is presumed by cryptozoologists that thunderbirds have a greater affinity for electricity and thus can control the inner electricity of the lightning snake. Lightning snakes have been observed passively presenting themselves as food for hungry thunderbirds.

Lightning snakes mate for life, and only reproduce once every few years. The female will lay around 300 eggs in a nest, of which only a few will hatch, and even fewer will grow to maturity. It usually takes around 20 to 25 years for a lightning snake to reach full maturity. Lightning snakes are long-lived; the oldest lightning snake on record was 137 years old when it was killed by poachers.

A juvenile lightning snake is called an elver. A group of lightning snakes is called a shoal.

HABITAT: Lightning snakes live in the coastal waters of Thunderbird Province. They are saltwater dwelling. They live in dens, or cubby holes formed under the ocean floor.

BIOLOGY: Lightning snakes have the same internal organs as the electric eel, only on a larger scale. Instead of 5,000 to 6,000 electroplaques, a lightning snake could have 20 times as many, in a much larger size. In most ways, they resemble their smaller knifefish brethren.

DIET: Lightning snakes are carnivorous, eating most sea life including smaller whales and wasco. First-born hatchlings often eat other eggs and embryos from later clutches.

MAGICAL USES: Lightning snakes cannot be trained, and are too large to display in aquariums, much less use as pets or familiars. They cannot be used for transportation, as they would fry any riders. Their electroplaques can be used for a number of spells and potions. Their skin can be tanned and worn as a cloak that resists electrical attacks. Their bones can be used for the cores of wands. Their lightning can be stored in terracotta jars as primitive batteries.

Among the regular atrocities of Jack Slager was the creation of an artifact from electroplaques of the lightning snake that was reported to have fatally electrocuted six Marshals in pursuit of the fugitive. Since then, Marshals have "taken an interest" whenever lightning snake electroplaques are purchased, so when acquiring some expect a "friendly visit" from the puffed-up busybodies.

DEFENSE: Lightning snakes are best escaped from by a vertical retreat away from the water. Levitation is less desirable than flight, because a wizard levitating too close to the water may still be in range of the lightning snake's leap into the air. Most lightning snake components are leavings from when a thunderbird chooses them for their dinner. It has been speculated that a powerful enough cold spell, cast with precise timing, could imprison the lightning snake in a block of ice, but all attempts have failed.

LOUP-GAROU

Homo lupus loquax

FAMILY: *Chimerical Humanoid*
CLASSIFICATION: *Sapient*
MANIFESTATION: *Corporeal, Phasic*
PRONUNCIATION: *LŪga-rū*

Modern cryptozoologists now understand that loup-garoux (singular: loup-garou) are humans who have undergone a closely guarded ritual that bestows shape-changing abilities on its subject. It appears that the ability was discovered by accidental experimentation, or perhaps as a magical gift from an extra-planar creature, and is not the result of an infection, curse, or bite. Because loup-garoux had certain advantages, including superior hunting ability, greater body mass, and better control over their body temperature, this unique state was quite desirable, and the secret of the initiation ritual became jealously guarded.

The first known humans with this ability were known as Animoshinini or "Dog-man" in Algonquin, and tended to be revered for their incredible powers. With the arrival of European colonists came the re-appellation to the French term "loup-garou," along with a frenzy of fear and persecution, forcing many of them to hide their abilities. European colonists were familiar only with werewolves, or lycans, which they thought of as ferocious and murderous wolf-creatures that had terrorized their cities and countryside, and murdered (and eaten) innocent humans. This became particularly pronounced after the trial of Peter Stumpp in 1589, though the persecution of loup-garoux in North America reached its height around the same time as the Salem Witch Trials.

Loup-garoux are humans that have the ability to change their shape into that of a bipedal, wolf-like creature; gaining the strength, speed, agility, fierceness, superior hearing, and scent-tracking of their lupine brethren. The notable differences between a werewolf and a loup-garou is the origin of the shapeshifting ability, the extent to which it can be controlled, and the esteem granted to (or denied from) the individual. Candidates to become a loup-garou are carefully selected by lodges for membership, the main criteria ostensibly being heroic action and deeds; but the reality is that lodge membership is often nepotistic, and invitations to join a Lodge without a familial connection are quite rare. Loup-garoux are considered part of the Magimundi, since the manifestation is similar to the way magical abilities appear, and because most—though not all—loup-garoux also possess other magical talents.

In stark contrast to loup-garoux, werewolves are afflicted by the wolf-powers, which are thrust upon them through a curse, bite, scratch, or, some believe, as the result of a pact with a devil or demon. Generally, werewolves are at the mercy of the moon or other elements that make shapeshifting into their wolf form nearly impossible to resist. Werewolves also have a tendency to walk on all fours while loup-garoux always walk upright, even in wolf form.

While loup-garoux are, for all intents and purposes, humans with remarkable abilities, they are included in this volume to inform citizens of their bestial manifestations. Loup-garoux retain the ability to reason and reflect while in wolf-form, and in many instances, to speak (hence the Latin name *Lupus loquax*), although the anatomy of a wolf's mouth prevents speech intelligible to the average human or mage.

A full-grown loup-garou can stand as tall as 9 feet. Their bodies tend to be completely fur-covered in wolf-form, and the fur color is similar to the hair color of their human counterpart. Humans who dye their hair affect the color of their wolf fur as well. Loup-garou faces are distinctly wolf-like, though they retain some human characteristics, particularly around the eyes. Loup-garou front paws retain some of the

What baseless slander! Clearly the author is speaking from a place of jealousy. To my considerable experience Lodges continually select and promote only the most worthy candidates for membership and it would be my absolute honor to be welcomed by one.

prehensile ability of human hands, though not with the same level of dexterity.

Nemort creatures fear a loup-garou and will scramble to distance themselves. Nemorts can sense or somehow magically divine that a particular human is a loup-garou or lycan, and they fear the former far more than the latter.

A loup-garou can change shape at will, and is known to shift into wolf form in response to threats. Physically more powerful than any human, a loup-garou is a formidable opponent who has the instinctual ability to coordinate attacks with with other loup-garoux. This uncanny ability, believed to be a sort of telepathy unique to loup-garoux, is the subject of much speculation among the Magimundi, although ethical concerns constrain what research may be done.

Since the ritual of initiation into a lodge is made no earlier than when the candidate reaches adulthood, there is no term for a juvenile loup-garou; it is considered derogatory to use the term "pup." Some people call a group of loup-garoux a "pack", but this term has begun to fall into disfavor, and may be considered derogatory as well. The general loup-garou community has suggested using the term "lodge" as a collective noun.

HABITAT: Loup-garoux can live anywhere in North America, but are clustered particularly in Destiny Province and Mishipeshu north of the Great Lakes. A smaller, but growing, contingent can be found in Solaris. When in wolf-form, loup-garoux seem to prefer wooded areas, where they can satisfy their urge to hunt

BIOLOGY: When in human form, a loup-garou is physically indistinguishable from another human. However, one loup-garou can detect another loup-garou by a particular scent issuing from the area of the neck. As mentioned above, nemort creatures can also sense the presence of a loup-garou. When in wolf form, a loup-garou retains injuries or distinguishing characteristics of the human. For example, a loup-garou missing a hand in human form would shift to a wolf missing a paw.

If a loup-garou dies in its wolf-form, the body remains a wolf. If it dies in its human form, the body remains a human.

DIET: Loup-garoux have a powerful urge to hunt, and many believe this drives them to change shape. They prefer to hunt large mammals such as deer, antelope, elk, and moose, though they will fell smaller prey such as foxes and hares. Loup-garoux eat mainly meat, though they also eat raw and unprocessed natural foods, such as seeds, nuts, berries, and some types of bark.

The Paleo diet phenomenon that has spilled into the Mundane world is believed to be derived from the loup-garou diet. Wish I had thought to market that.

MAGICAL USES: Cryptozoologists have been studying loup-garoux for centuries attempting to figure out the secrets of their ability to coordinate attacks without using speech, believing it it be a kind of telepathy. Many loup-garoux also are immune to known forms of mind magic, or they possess the ability to shield their minds from attempts to enter it. This makes them very difficult to prosecute by Magimundi Marshals and also makes them valuable as assassins or agents. In the 1950s, some young adult loup-garoux were "selected for a special program" in a Magimundi medical complex where they underwent a series of tests to understand their telepathy and shape-shifting trait. The program was shut down after 10 years of research, after protests from activists. A loup-garou tail supposedly taken from its body in wolf-form circulated among the Magimundi artifact underground in the 19th century, and was said to be a talisman of great and unknown power. It has not been seen in more than 100 years, and is generally considered lost or destroyed. Counterfeit loup-garou tails poached from North American wolves are often sold to gullible magi hoping to increase their power.

Note: Loup-garoux are human beings with the trained ability to shapeshift. Harvesting a loup-garou for parts carries with it the same penalties as harvesting a human for parts.

DEFENSE: Loup-garoux in their wolf-form have skin that is nigh-impervious to mundane blades and bullets, and they appear to be immune to all forms of incendiary magic. Loup-garoux are stronger, faster, possess more stamina, and have better tracking senses than ordinary humans. A physical altercation with one is ill-advised. Because loup-garoux retain their ability to reason and, to some extent, to speak while in wolf-form, bargaining with a hostile loup-garou is considered the best course of action. Another defense is the *Cacaphonio* spell, which conjures a series of loud and confusing noises that disrupt the loup-garou's keen hearing and provides an opportunity for escape.

MANNEGISHI

Mannegishi sexdactylous

FAMILY: *Humanoid*
CLASSIFICATION: Para-sapient
MANIFESTATION: *Phasic*
PRONUNCIATION: *ma-ni-GESH-ē*

The Mannegishi (singular the same) are mysterious trickster creatures that inhabit the northern regions of North America. They are humanoid, with very thin and lanky arms and legs, six digits on each hand and foot, and large heads that lack a nose. The Mannegishi live on the banks of rivers or in dams on the river itself, and one of their chiefest delights is to capsize the boats of people as they travel across areas of rapids, particularly over rocks and shoals. They can also wreak havoc during portage between bodies of water, upsetting crafts, and spoiling or stealing the goods being carried.

Mannegishi are an aquatic species, and spend most of their time in in the river. They absorb oxygen from the water through their skin, similar to one method of how amphibians breathe.

The Mannegishi are adept crafters, and use stone as their primary medium. They have been known to carve pictographs into stone, and even create canoes from it.

They nest within existing structures such as caves, or build their own dwellings that from the outside appear to nothing more than a pile of rocks. Some have been found near the Inunnguaq in Mishipeshu Province, always near water. They can disrupt teleportation spells if they interfere during the casting procedure. It is also believed they can communicate via telepathy, and possess either an uncanny intuition or at least a marginal ability to penetrate human minds.

Mannegishi will trade with magi, although a bargain with a Mannegishi is a serious undertaking, similar to that of negotiating with a leprechaun. Wizards among the indigenous North American magi bargained with the Mannegishi for peaceful coexistence, and safety of person and property. Over time they have created a tenuous trust. Mannegishi appear to especially favor human luxuries such as tobacco and furs. Many wizard coureur de bois, including Jean Bicolet and Étienne Brûlé, are also known to have traded with the Mannegishi. When bartering with Mannegishi, it is advised to have the proper runic wards to protect one's mind from intrusion.

A juvenile Mannegishi is called a child. The collective noun for a group of Mannegishi is a crowd.

HABITAT: The Mannegishi are almost exclusively found in Canada. They do not like warm weather, and will stay in the water to keep themselves cool during the summer.

I have never once found evidence of these creatures apart from the occasional stone carving, and I am convinced they do not exist. I am halfway to thinking they are invention of the author and entirely fictional.

BIOLOGY: An adult Mannegishi can grow to four to five feet in height. They are amphibious in nature, and must keep their skin moist to survive. The Mannegishi are normally corporeal, but it is believed that they may turn spectral at times to travel.

DIET: Mannegishi are omnivorous. Although they tend toward a herbivorous diet of river plants, they will consume fish and insects at times.

MAGICAL USES: Mannegishi skin can be used to form waterproof clothing. Their eyes can be used for divination. Their finger bones can be used as wands. Other parts of the Mannegishi can be used for potions, charms, and talismans.

DEFENSE: Mannegishi have never been known to engage in violence. If a person approaches their whereabouts with malicious intent, they are presumed to take measures so that they cannot be found by the aggressor.

MERMAID

Mulier piscus

FAMILY: *Ichthyolios-Humanoid Chimera*
CLASSIFICATION: *Sapient*
MANIFESTATION: *Corporeal*
PRONUNCIATION: *MER-mād*

Mermaids are water dwelling chimerical creatures with a humanoid head and torso, and the lower extremities of a fish. There are both saltwater and freshwater mermaids. All mermaids appear to have a single gender. The secret of mermaid reproduction has not yet been unlocked by the Magimundi.

Mermaids are sentient and sapient, and many seafaring magical communities have treaties with the merfolk. They enjoy various manufactured goods, and give pearls and various treasures of the sea in return.

Mermaids are similar to their European cousins, the Sirens, but do not share their ability to mesmerise through song.

The tribes of freshwater mermaids living in the Great Lakes are currently at war with each other, and although the conflict can be traced back generations, those on the outside do not have a firm understanding of what precipitated the original feud. The war tends to be cold, only to break out into active fighting every 5-10 years or so. The last major mermaid battle of the Great Lakes was in 2007.

A juvenile mermaid is called a child. The collective noun for a group of mermaids is a splash.

HABITAT: Salt water mermaids live in tribes along the coasts of temperate climes. There are many notable tribes of Atlantic mermaids ranging as far north as Bermuda, and as far south as French Guiana. There are several tribes of freshwater mermaids who live in the Great Lakes of North America.

River mermaids have gone extinct in North America due to human pollution and destruction of habitat. South American river mermaids still exist in some of the more remote parts of the Amazon River.

BIOLOGY: Mermaids have one of the more fascinating biologies of any cryptozoological creature, as they possess dual mammalian and piscine nature. They may breathe air, like sea mammals, but also have gills which they may use to filter water for oxygen. It is presumed that they reproduce like fish based on dissection of mermaid bodies, but this remains theoretical.

DIET: Mermaids are omnivorous, and subsist on seaweed and sea creatures, including fish and crustaceans. They can digest human food as well and especially appreciate a home cooked meal and chocolate.

MAGICAL USES: Mermaid tongues and scales have magical properties, and can be used for a variety of potions and charms. Mermaid hair is a common component for the cores of wands. Other mermaid organs have magical properties and are quite useful.

Note: Mermaids are considered a protected species by the North American Council of Five. They are considered sentient beings with intelligence equal to humans. Harvesting a mermaid for parts carries with it the same penalties as harvesting a human for parts.

DEFENSE: Mermaids are both intelligent and magical, and should you find yourself facing the ire of one of these creatures, prepare yourself for a variety of offensive tactics, both martial and magical. The single best defense is to communicate diplomatically, and offer gifts, in order to be welcomed safely. If you are approaching their territory when they are at war however, you may find your property confiscated, in which case your best choice is to remain stoic and quiet, writing off the loss. Mermaids at war will gladly kill you, rather than listen to you complain.

My case in the Destiny Court system where I assert that when acting in self defense, one can claim the body of the mermaid attacker as property is still ongoing. When I win, I will be putting my rightfully claimed artifacts up for auction.

MISHIPESHU

Lynx subaqua

FAMILY: *Mammalian*
CLASSIFICATION: *Semi-sapient*
MANIFESTATION: *Corporeal*
PRONUNCIATION: *MISH-ē-PESH-ū*

The Mishipeshu, commonly known as the Underwater Panther, is a very powerful magical creature native to the Great Lakes area of the United States and Canada. Mishipeshu translates into "the Great Lynx". They live on the islands in the Great Lakes. They are formidable fighters, and are known to be highly dangerous.

Mishipeshu and thunderbirds are mortal enemies, and will fight to the death whenever they encounter one another. This seems to be instinctual and impossible to stop once started. Thunderbirds and mishipeshu both appear to wield elemental magic, and the clash of air and water in their various forms, combined with the physical combat of the two creatures creates quite a spectacle.

Mishipeshu are equally at home in the water or on land. They are excellent swimmers, but they also can walk along the bottom of lakes if they choose. The mishipeshu possess the ability to breathe underwater, as well as to walk through snow without leaving tracks (although the mechanism making either of these possible is unknown).

Mishipeshu live in family groups with an alpha male and several females. When male mishipeshu reach adulthood, they start challenging the existing alpha for dominance of the chain. The loser of this challenge is forced to leave the group and become a solitary hunter.

A juvenile mishipeshu is called a kitten. The word mishipeshu is both singular and plural, like sheep or fish. The collective noun for a group of mishipeshu is a chain.

HABITAT: The mishipeshu live in small family groups in the islands of the Great Lakes.

BIOLOGY: Mishipeshu have the head and paws of a giant cat, the antlers of a deer, dagger-like spikes running along its back and tail, and is completely covered in scales.

DIET: Mishipeshu are carnivores. They will eat small mammals, birds, and fish, but prefer to hunt larger mammals, such as reindeer, deer, and elk. Mishipeshu have been known to hunt and consume mermaids as well.

MAGICAL USES: The pelt of the mishipeshu can be made into magical clothing that is naturally resistant to water. The antlers and spikes are used to make wands. Its ears can be made into potent hearing charms. The breath of the mishipeshu can be collected and used in a potion that allows the imbiber to breathe underwater for approximately an hour.

DEFENSE: No wizard has ever survived the attack of a mishipeshu. Mishipeshu have been witnessed taking great wounds and losing copious amounts of their luminescent blue-silver blood, without so much as slowing down. Simply put, none but a thunderbird may hope to kill a mishipeshu in open combat. Any parts of a Mishipeshu that are used as spell components are presumed to have been naturally shed over the course of its life, the remains of the dominance conflict between males, or harvested from the carcass after a battle with a thunderbird. It has been noted that when in the presence of a mishipeshu, dropping to one's knees and touching one's forehead to the ground in obeisance has, with notable consistency, meant being spared harm. When rising after the great creature leaves, this respectful approach may result in being left a gift of uncut precious stones, or thunderbird components like feathers or talons.

I have visited and paid my respects to mishipeshu on four separate occasions and have never once received a gift, though every other member of my expedition did. I will not be trying a fifth time. These creatures are jerks.

THE MOTHMAN

Homo lepidoptera

FAMILY: *Humanoid*
CLASSIFICATION: *Para-Sapient*
MANIFESTATION: *Corporeal*
PRONUNCIATION: *MOTH-man*

Roanoke colonist and mage Thomas Crowley was a talented and clever shapeshifter who had, over the course of years, learned to take the form of over twelve different animals, including birds and fish. Working in secret, he devised a ritual to take his abilities even further.

According to his notes, "we have conquered the beasts of the field and the air, but what of the wonders of the world beyond?" And so, in 1588, Elder Crowley attempted to transform himself into an angel. It should be noted at this time that there has never been physical evidence for the existence of angels, but Crowley was undeterred.

Unfortunately, the spell—now lost—misfired, transforming Crowley into a hideous, vicious, winged man and addling his mind in the process. While he did show himself capable of speech, his behavior clearly demonstrated a savage and bestial nature. He either fled from the Roanoke Colony, was cast out, and traveled west into the wilds of what would eventually become West Virginia.

Besides transforming his body and mind, the spell seems to have made Crowley immortal, or at least unageing. He is still sighted occasionally by magi and mundanes alike, and has been given the nickname of "the Mothman."

The Mothman lives a solitary and feral life in the wilds of West Virginia, although he is occasionally visited by magi from Virginia Isle, for reasons unknown except to them. His exact biology is unknown, although he appears as a large bipedal humanoid with a 10 foot wingspan. The wings of the Mothman are feathered, and allow him to fly short distances.

The head of the Mothman is entirely hairless, with slits for his eyes and nose, and a mouth full of sharp pointed teeth. His skin is an iridescent white and his eyes glow red.

The Mothman does not care for human companionship, and will attack most magi who seek him out. He is highly resistant to most magics and should only be approached with great caution.

After the fifth "friendly visit" to "Just see how your expedition was coming along, Mr. Diego," from Cryptozoologist Wizards from Virginia Isle and locals, I got the distinct impression that they did not wish me to find the Lair of the Mothman. Well, I know when I'm being treated unfairly, so the search has been postponed indefinitely.

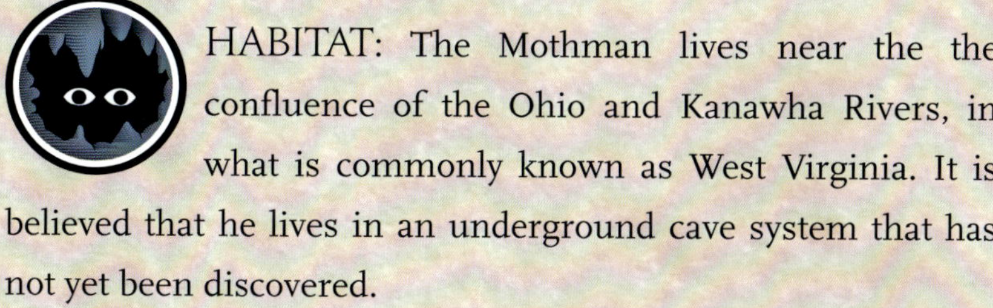

HABITAT: The Mothman lives near the the confluence of the Ohio and Kanawha Rivers, in what is commonly known as West Virginia. It is believed that he lives in an underground cave system that has not yet been discovered.

BIOLOGY: The exact biology of the Mothman is unknown, but it is believed that his internal biology is human, with the addition of feathered wings.

DIET: The Mothman is believed to be omnivorous, hunting small mammals and deer, and also feeding on wild fruits, nuts, and berries.

MAGICAL USES: The artificers of Virginia Isle are able to craft fine wands with cores that they claim come from the feathers of the Mothman. It is unknown if that is the truth, but there is no reason to doubt them.

DEFENSE: The Mothman is preternaturally fast, and can fly. It has sharp claws and teeth, and will attack on sight. It is resistant to most spells, but will flee if outnumbered. Wounds caused by the Mothman often become infected, and require magical treatments to heal properly.

NAGUAL

Homo sapiens chimerical

FAMILY: *Chimerical Humanoid*
CLASSIFICATION: *Sapient*
MANIFESTATION: *Corporeal*
PRONUNCIATION: *na-GŪL*

A nagual is not a beast. Nagualli are human magi who are born with the power to shift themselves into one or more animal forms. The most common form of a nagual is usually a large cat, such as a jaguar or puma, but talented nagualli can also transform into other animals. While mammal forms are the most common, birds are not unheard of, and it is theoretically possible for a nagual to turn into a cryptozoological creature, although to date there have been no credibly documented instances of this occurring.

Nagualli are accepted into the Magimundi community and have the same rights and privileges as any other person. That being said, there are those who consider nagualli to be "bestial demi-humans who only pretend to be people." This bigotry was especially prevalent until the mid-nineteenth century, and has no place in modern magical sensibilities.

Despite mundane claims to the existence of such things as "conservation of matter," when a nagual transforms into an animal, their size and age translates commensurately: a human will become an animal of a size and age proportionate to the life-cycle of that animal. For example, a large man is likely to become a large bear when he transforms; similarly, a young adult human will become a juvenile panther cub.

Nagualli are limited to one distinct animal shape per species when they shift. For example, a nagual who takes the shape of a wolfhound

will be unable to take the shape of any other dog, or one with a bengal tiger shape will be unable to take the form of a siberian tiger.
Likewise, the animal they turn into will have distinct markings which cannot be altered when they transform, nor can a nagual alter their human appearance through use of their shapeshifting.

Injuries or disabilities that a nagual sustains while human remain with them when they transform; a human with an injured arm would turn into a bird with an injured wing. The extent of the injuries are made proportional with the change, just like all other variables.

It is vanishingly rare for a nagual to be able to transform into more than two animals (aside from their base human form). There have always been rumors of the poly-nagual, who can transform into any animal, but such a being is more likely legend than reality.

Nagual inherit all the instincts of their specific animal when they transform, but not necessarily the skill to use them effectively. As with young animals, the mage must practice their abilities until they become proficient. While transformed, magi eat the usual diet of the animal they have become, and some even come to enjoy it. The quantity of the food in their stomachs will be transformed in terms of amount, but not in nature: a belly full of raw meat as a panther means a belly full of raw meat as a human.

When in their animal form, naguallі are sterile; they can perform mating functions with other animals, but will not produce any offspring. If a nagual is pregnant in her human form, the fetus is not represented in the nagual's animal form and is completely unaffected by her time as the animal. A nagual in labor will be unable to shift into animal form until after she has given birth.

Naguallі retain their human intelligence while in animal form; however, the longer they stay in the animal form, the more likely they are to begin forgetting their humanity. There are cases of a nagual becoming trapped in their animal form permanently after having gone too long without taking their human shape.

HABITAT: Nagualli can be found in any Magimundi community. They are people. It is possible for a nagual to transform into an animal outside its native habitat.

BIOLOGY: When in the form of a person, a nagual is biologically identical to a person; when in animal form, they are biologically identical to that animal. When a nagual dies, it returns to human form.

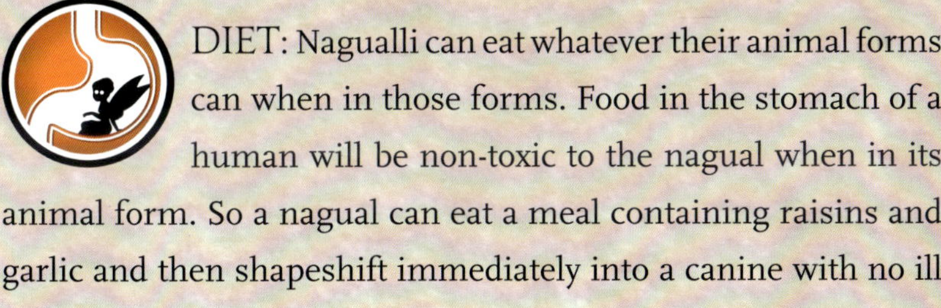

DIET: Nagualli can eat whatever their animal forms can when in those forms. Food in the stomach of a human will be non-toxic to the nagual when in its animal form. So a nagual can eat a meal containing raisins and garlic and then shapeshift immediately into a canine with no ill effect.

MAGICAL USES: An odd side effect of the shapeshifting process is that none of the products of the animal the nagual turns into (teeth, skin, claws, feathers, etc.) can be used for magical purposes. It's almost as if magic itself considers that cheating.

DEFENSE: As a remnant from the days of persecution, a spell had been developed to lock a shapeshifter into their present form for a brief time, which greatly assisted the Wizard-hunters of nagualli, but it is the opinion of this author that no good can come from the sharing of this spell. Naguals are human magi, and therefore the best defense is respect and courtesy.

And it's the opinion of this commentator that you are WRONG, Castellaw. The spell is Pejig Pàgingwe.

NÛÑNË'HÏ

Homo paulum

FAMILY: *Humanoid*
CLASSIFICATION: *Para-sapient*
MANIFESTATION: *Phasic*
PRONUNCIATION: *nun-NĀ-hē*

The nunnehi are a subterranean guardian-spirit people who live in the southern Appalachian mountains. They build large villages within the mountains themselves, especially preferring the higher peaks.

Nunnehi have formed their own communities within the earth, and have been trading with humans for centuries. They especially favor people of Cherokee descent, but will deal with anyone who treats them honorably. They have a particular distrust of pale-skinned people, stemming from the mistreatment of the Cherokee by white colonists.

The nunnehi were trading partners, allies, and spiritual guardians of the Cherokee people who lived near the Appalachian mountains until 1838. For nearly 30 years after the forced relocation of the Cherokee in 1838, the nunnehi retreated into their underground settlements, and refused any contact with the outside world. The only exception to this rule was their decision to aid in the fight against the Akeldama revenant attack in 1864.

Nunnehi have some natural shape-shifting and phasic abilities. They can appear indistinguishable from human beings, or they can appear as tiny humans ranging from 12 to 60 inches tall. They can also evade detection, both magical and mundane. It is suspected that they may take other forms, and that the shape of humanity is not their true form, but no other form has ever been seen or recorded.

Visitors to their underground villages report that they seem to live in a manner similar to humans. They even seem to have a system of internal government, laws, and communications between villages.

Nunnehi will occasionally allow humans to come live with them. The nunnehi grow their own food in their underground villages, and it seems to prevent both aging and disease. Humans can eat nunnehi food as well, and enjoy the benefits of it, but at the cost of never being able to consume a normal human diet again as their bodies will simply reject it. Nunnehi are as varied as humans are. They tend to appear in traditional Cherokee clothing, but they can appear in more modern day mundane or Wizardly clothing if they so wish. They are very intelligent, and sharp traders. Their fighters are excellent and will always defeat a human fighter in one-on-one combat; however, they can be overwhelmed by groups of human fighters. The nunnehi can fight while invisible, and make formidable enemies when angered.

Nunnehi value honesty and compassion above all. They are known for taking in lost and sick humans, allowing them to live in their underground villages, and to return home to visit when they wish. Nunnehi have no desire to join the above-ground world and live among the Magimundi as some vampires do, but they are willing to deal with those who treat others fairly.

A juvenile nunnehi is called a child. The collective nouns that are used for humans are also used for nunnehi.

HABITAT: Nunnehi live in underground villages in the southern Appalachian mountains in the Solaris Province. They also can live in single-family underground dwellings called townhomes.

BIOLOGY: Internally, nunnehi have the same structure as humans. They do need to breathe and eat, although they can only digest their own food.

DIET: Nunnehi eat a special food of their own design, most likely a magical kind of fungus, that they can shape and season to resemble any human food they wish (cakes are often reported).

MAGICAL USES: Nunnehi body parts or blood can be used in any spell or potion that would require the same parts from a human. In that case, the duration of the spell is increased fivefold.

Nunnehi are willing to trade with humans. They have many interesting magical components and plants that are not available elsewhere. They are not interested in money, but are interested in raw materials, luxury goods, and especially the fine arts, as they do not have any artists of their own.

Note: Nunnehi are considered a protected species by the North American Council of Five. They are considered sentient beings with intelligence equal to humans. Harvesting a nunnehi for parts carries with it the same penalties as harvesting a human for parts.

I intend to personally lead an expedition to visit and trade with these creatures, and find out for myself if Castellaw speaks the truth on them. Interested backers and interns should contact me before the expedition's roster is full.

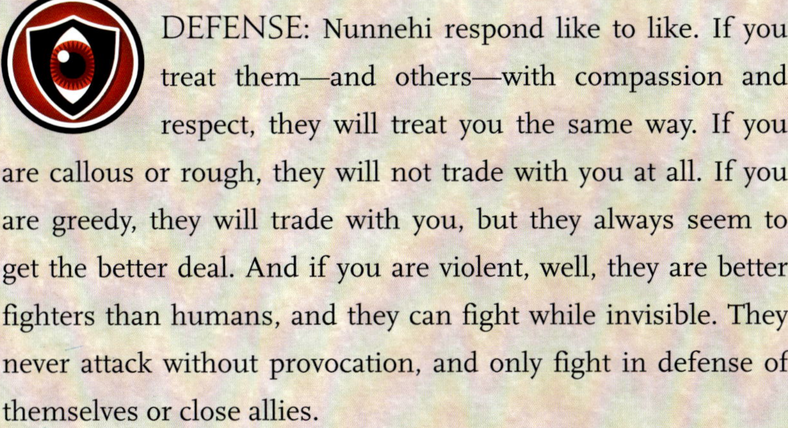

DEFENSE: Nunnehi respond like to like. If you treat them—and others—with compassion and respect, they will treat you the same way. If you are callous or rough, they will not trade with you at all. If you are greedy, they will trade with you, but they always seem to get the better deal. And if you are violent, well, they are better fighters than humans, and they can fight while invisible. They never attack without provocation, and only fight in defense of themselves or close allies.

Nunnehi can make themselves entirely undetectable to human perception, magical or otherwise. This would make them excellent spies, if they did not find the concept dishonorable.

THE 113-YEAR LOCUST

Schistocerca centum-tredecim

FAMILY: *Insectoid*
CLASSIFICATION: *Non-sapient*
MANIFESTATION: *Corporeal*
PRONUNCIATION: *thē/WUN-HUN-dred-an(d)-THUR(T)-tēn/yir/LŌ-kest*

The 113-year locust is a type of grasshopper that lays dormant for 112 years, and then, for exactly one day in the summer, erupts seemingly out of nowhere to swarm and devour their chosen foodstuff.

There are 112 different subspecies of the 113-year locust on record, and they cycle through periods of activity at a rate of one subspecies per year, with the exception of the 113th year. For example: subspecies 1 may be active in 1866, subspecies 2 in 1867, subspecies 3 in 1868 and so on until the 113th year in which no locusts swarm. Each swarm of locusts will feed on something different from that of the previous year. Luckily, records are complete enough that we can anticipate their arrival.

The locusts will swarm for one day, in a small area in Mishipeshu Province. The swarm is typically not larger than a half mile in diameter, but may be so thick with locusts that the swarm becomes visually impenetrable.

The swarming usually happens between the 8th-21st of June, but as the locusts seem to be operating on a lunar calendar, the swarming occurs in mid-July at irregular (but predictable) intervals. The first signs of the swarming are a loud buzzing sound just before dawn. The swarm erupts with the first rays of the sun's light and ends abruptly at sunset.

The swarm never appears in the same exact place twice, but their appearance can still be predicted with some accuracy. If there is no foodstuff of the appropriate kind where the swarm appears, it will travel toward the closest food source. Sometimes, the swarm will split into smaller groups if there are multiple food sources nearby.

Each of the 112 sub-species prefer a different food. Some are easily satisfied, with preferences for such things as mammalian flesh, plant-life or air. Others have a more specialized diet and require eyes, grasses, freshly-baked pastries, or hoop snake stingers. Yet another category feed only on the esoteric, devouring intangibles like sunlight, mortality, love, time, or fear. It is beyond the scope of this book to list all 112 different subspecies of locust. I suggest you purchase my companion book, *Unlocking The Locust (The 113 Year Locust in Depth)* for more information.

All attempts made to eradicate these vermin have been unsuccessful, due in part to the lack of information about where the locusts actually go when dormant. Unlike other locusts, the 113-year locust does not simply burrow underground, but seems to wink out of existence entirely between cycles. Various theories have been offered regarding the nature of their disappearance, including suggestions that the locusts travel to another part of the world, another plane of existence, or even that they are not bound by the laws of linear time.

Tests have conclusively shown that a different subspecies of locust is active each year of the cycle. Dissections have informed us that there is a marked difference between the digestive systems of those locusts that eat abstractions, and those that eat physical matter. Also, cryptozoologists have had some success marking individual locusts and tracking their appearance to exactly 113 years after their last sighting. Legend has it that the missing 113th subspecies of locust fed on swarming grasshoppers and that it cannibalized itself to death. It is therefore possible that given time, a new subspecies will rise to take its place. Little is known about how the 113-year locust reproduce. There is no term for a juvenile. The collective noun is a swarm.

HABITAT: The swarm appears in a small area of of very arable farmland in Mishipeshu Province and can travel from there. It is unknown where the locusts go when dormant.

BIOLOGY: For the most part, the locusts resemble the common American grasshopper, especially in size and shape. However, each sub-species is adapted to feed upon their preferred food source.

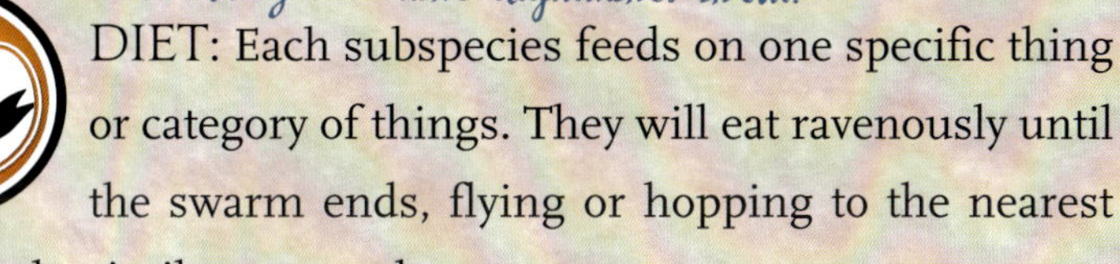

DIET: Each subspecies feeds on one specific thing or category of things. They will eat ravenously until the swarm ends, flying or hopping to the nearest food supply, similar to grasshoppers.

MAGICAL USES: The individual members of the swarm can be killed and used for spells and potions, although they are not any better for this purpose than the common grasshopper.

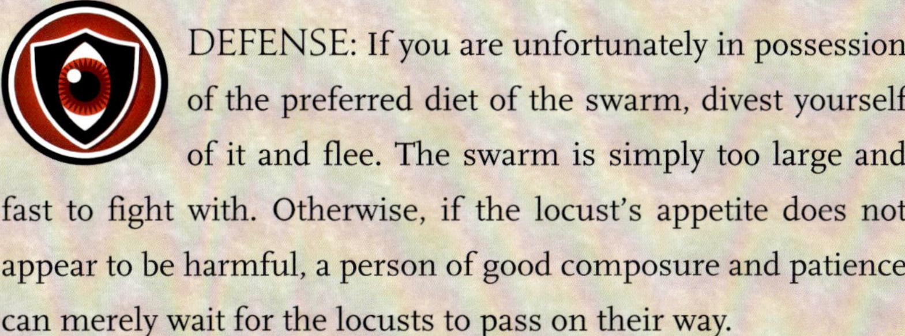

DEFENSE: If you are unfortunately in possession of the preferred diet of the swarm, divest yourself of it and flee. The swarm is simply too large and fast to fight with. Otherwise, if the locust's appetite does not appear to be harmful, a person of good composure and patience can merely wait for the locusts to pass on their way.

POLHAPPLER'S MANTIS

Mantis colossaeus

FAMILY: *Insectoid*
CLASSIFICATION: *Non-sapient*
MANIFESTATION: *Corporeal*
PRONUNCIATION: *pol-HAP-lers/MAN-tis*

The Polhappler's mantis is a mantis approximately the size of a small pony. It is native to the North American Midwest and South central plains areas, as well as parts of Central America. It is employed in agriculture, both as a work animal and transportation. They are occasionally eaten by humans, but they are more commonly used as a source of food for livestock and pets.

A Polhappler's mantis has a triangular head atop a fully articulated neck, which allows it to rotate its head nearly 270 degrees. It has two raptorial front legs, and four posterior legs. It has a set of four flat translucent wings. A mature female Polhappler's mantis grows to about 8 feet long and weighs 250 lbs. The male is smaller than the female, growing to about 6 feet long and weighing about 175 lbs. All Polhappler's mantises are capable of bearing many times their own weight.

Polhappler's mantises cannot fly, but they can jump over 20 feet in the air. They can also perform complex maneuvers while in the air, and "mantis rodeos" are a common sight in Baja Province. However, the most useful feature of the jumps are that a simple spell performed while at the apex of the jump can cause the mantis, its rider, and cargo to teleport up to 100 miles away. This allows a very effective system of long distance transportation for those who can get the hang of riding the mantis.

Polhappler's mantises need to be gentled before they can successfully be ridden. There are many terrible (and humorous) accounts of would-be riders sent flying into the next field when they attempted to mount a supposedly docile mantis. The process of accustoming a mantis to a rider takes time, patience, and the use of positive reinforcement, and is the subject of many books.

Polhappler's mantises can also be trained to pull a cart or plow. Such mantises usually have their wings clipped to prevent damaging the cart should the mantis startle or jump. For some reason, the mantis is unable or unwilling to jump if its wings are clipped.

Polhappler's mantises live for about five years. Females lay eggs each fall, typically 10-15 in number, and if fertilized, they will hatch in the spring. A female Polhappler's mantis does perform sexual cannibalism. It is unknown exactly what purpose this serves, although it has been speculated that the male cannot finish the act unless its head is removed from its body. Polhappler's mantises become dormant in the winter when the temperature drops below 40 degrees. In warmer climates, they may not become dormant at all.

Polhappler's mantises have excellent camouflage and can even change their color and markings like a chameleon. When at rest and not hiding, they are bright green. A Polhappler's mantis will molt every other month in its first year as it grows to adulthood. Polhappler's mantises do not have wings until adulthood.

A juvenile Polhappler's mantis is called a nymph. The collective noun for a group of Polhappler's mantises is a swarm.

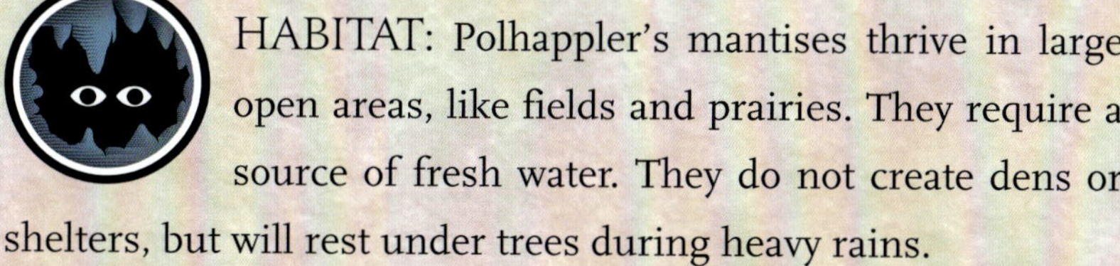

HABITAT: Polhappler's mantises thrive in large open areas, like fields and prairies. They require a source of fresh water. They do not create dens or shelters, but will rest under trees during heavy rains.

BIOLOGY: Polhappler's mantises are similar to the common praying mantis, although much larger. Adults have four non-functional wings. The necks of the Polhappler's mantis are more articulated than other mantises, allowing them a farther range of vision.

DIET: Wild Polhappler's mantises are carnivorous ambush predators. They will eat insects, as well as small mammals, birds, and fish.

MAGICAL USES: Polhappler's mantises are used for transportation, entertainment, and as draft animals, particularly on the large industrial magiflora farms. They are edible, although they are usually used for animal feed. Fried or grilled Polhappler's mantis legs are a popular food at Magimundi county fairs. The antennae of the Polhappler's mantis can be fashioned into a wand. Their molted skin, once properly charmed, can be made into socks that allow the wearer to jump up to 12 feet.

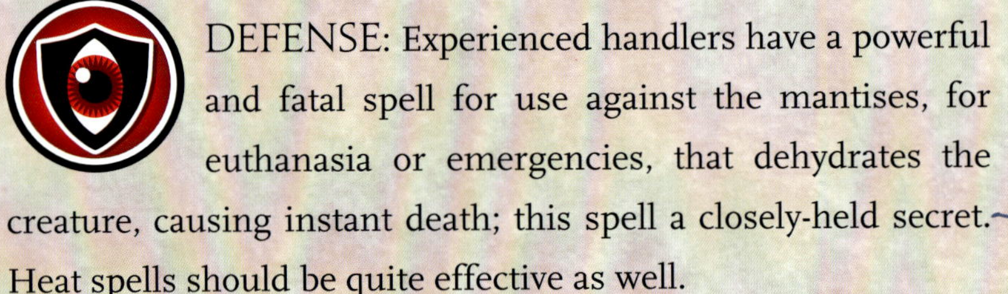

DEFENSE: Experienced handlers have a powerful and fatal spell for use against the mantises, for euthanasia or emergencies, that dehydrates the creature, causing instant death; this spell a closely-held secret. Heat spells should be quite effective as well.

The spell is kàpakamigà. I swear, Castellaw wasn't even trying to disseminate this information.

PUKWUDGIE

Homo fraxinus minutus

FAMILY: *Arboreal Humanoid*
CLASSIFICATION: *Para-sapient*
MANIFESTATION: *Corporeal*
PRONUNCIATION: *puk-WUJ-ē*

A pukwudgie, or pok-wejee-man, is a small arboreal spirit similar to a gnome or pixie. Made of the bark of an ash tree, they stand 2-3 feet in height and resemble short, flat humans. A new pukwudgie is created when an ash tree sloughs off some of its bark in a process known as pukwudgination. Pukwudgies are only created from the ash tree, and only in the Destiny and Mishipeshu Provinces, as far west as the Great Lakes.

Pukwudgies are mischievous protectors of the forest. According to legend, they were once friendly toward humans, but as settlers started deforestation, the pukwudgies turned hostile. Pukwudgies have been known to disable logging equipment, and are definitely responsible for at least ten deaths during the construction of the Erie Canal.

Pukwudgies are technically genderless, but have traditionally been referred to as male. Pukwudgies absorb carbon dioxide and "exhale" oxygen through their skin. They also absorb nutrients through their feet by means of tiny rootlets.

Pukwudgies live in small groups, usually around 6-10 individuals. They seem to act like extended families, but they do not actually care for each other, raise each other, or have true parents or children. Pukwudgies rarely gather together in groups of more than 11 or 12.

Pukwudgies exhibit many supernatural abilities: they can roll themselves into a ball to travel along the forest floor, flatten themselves around the base of a tree and vanish from sight, shoot venomous thorns from their "hands", create minor illusions, and even control the souls of those they killed and send them to perform simple errands.

It is generally considered bad luck to see a pukwudgie. They have no love of humans, and will try to find a way to hurt or kill you. While they are considered sapient creatures, they are not protected by edict and may be harvested for magical components.

There is no such thing as a juvenile pukwudgie. A group of pukwudgies is called a grove.

HABITAT: Pukwudgies live in small dens in the base of ash trees in the forests of the northeast. They require this habitat and will die in captivity.

BIOLOGY: Pukwudgies are living, mobile ash tree bark, and as such they have no internal organs. They possess retractable roots in their feet by which they absorb water and nutrients from the earth.

DIET: Pukwudgies are autotrophic, requiring only carbon dioxide, sunlight, water, and a few key nutrients to survive. They produce oxygen as a side-effect of their photosynthesis. The few inorganic compounds they cannot acquire through photosynthesis they obtain by temporarily putting down roots to feed. Pukwudgies are mobile, but must remain still to feed from their feet.

MAGICAL USES: The bark the pukwudgie is made of can be pressed into magical parchment. Pukwudgies can be rolled into a cylinder, glued together, and used for wands. Pukwudgies will not work with humans to become familiars.or neonates.

A permanently imprisoned creature used as a wand? And people suggest that I'm amoral!

DEFENSE: Pukwudgies are best left alone. Mundane or magical humans who cross a pukwudgie will find themselves the targets of persistent mischief at the hands of the wronged pukwudgie, which may include physical harm and "accidental" death such as being pushed from a cliff. Pukwudgies are vulnerable when they must stop to feed through their feet. A dehydration spell effect will prove fatal to a pukwudgie if hit directly. A wind spell (*Flabrum Diabolicum*) may be effective at temporarily blowing them off course. Planting an ash tree in the wronged pukwudgie's honor may also stave the mischievous hostility.

REVENANT

Homo mortis

FAMILY: *Nemort*
CLASSIFICATION: *Para-sapient*
MANIFESTATION: *Corporeal, Phasic*
PRONUNCIATION: RE-ve-nent

A revenant is a reanimated corpse or spirit, usually brought back by a necromantic ritual. Revenants are created in order to perform a specific task set by the Wizard. `Such a revenant may be just as intelligent as it was in life, but its will is usually bound by the Wizard who summons and controls it. Once the revenant completes its task, it disperses into dust and cannot be revived again. The specifics of the ritual, and the control of the corpse, are beyond the scope of this book.

Note: the creation of a revenant is considered a crime by the North American Council of Five, and is punishable by up to lifelong incarceration in Avernus Prison.

Revenants appear as living corpses. They have no bodily functions, including automatic respiration, digestion, circulation, procreation, or excretion. They are intelligent, and can speak if they choose to deliberately inhale and exhale. Most revenants are corporeal, but it is possible to create ones that are phasic as well.

Magi who are risen as revenants do not retain their magical powers. It is possible for exceptionally skilled necromancers to perform a ritual in which they sacrifice themselves and arise as powerful self-directed revenants, unaging and immortal except through extreme countermeasures. These self-made revenants are called liches. There have been perhaps as many as 5 known liches in all the recorded history of the Magimundi. Liches are usually hunted down and killed (using said extreme countermeasures) as soon as they are discovered, but one lich is known to have survived over 500 years.

It is possible for a revenant to form without necromantic interference. This occurs when a person dies under extreme and unusual violence, and if their body is intact, they may rise as revenants to take revenge on their murderers. While these natural revenants display all the normal features of the magically created revenants, they are considered non-sapient instead of para-sapient. Natural revenants can still be clever, and even use tools and weapons, but they do not display the same intelligence and self-awareness of magically created revenants.

Revenants break down over time, sloughing off limbs and organs which disintegrate unless magically refreshed. Should a mage who created a revenant die, the revenant will return to its original state as an inanimate corpse.

Revenants do not reproduce. The collective noun for a group of revenants is a horde.

Recent investigations have led Marshals and Cursebreakers to believe that the "natural" revenant phenomenon is anything but. I have been told in confidence that some evidence is beginning to show a pattern of a Wizard or Wizards seeking out the victims of notable crimes, raising the revenant and commanding the corpse to take vengeance. Far from "natural" if this is true.

HABITAT: Revenants do not have a habitat per se. Some stay near where they were created; others wander. They tend to avoid water as they can become waterlogged, which disrupts their ability to move and hastens their sloughing decay.

BIOLOGY: Revenants are magically animated human corpses. They do not have working internal organs, but they seem to be able to see, hear, and think. They have limited senses of taste, smell, and touch. They do not feel pain or discomfort. They do not get sick, and they do not heal injuries.

DIET: Revenants do not eat. They can take food into their mouths, and swallow it, but it inevitably sits in their stomachs and rots.

MAGICAL USES: There is no part of the revenant any more useful than the corresponding part taken from an ordinary corpse in terms of magical components, but the dust of disintegrated liches and revenants is a common ingredient in necromantic spells. It is rumored that the left arm bone from the great lich Pigishkanàbide was removed, preserved and fashioned into a wand, but this is likely legend.

In any case, necromancers have used revenants as servants for centuries. Any possible use that a revenant could be put to—house servant, transportation, energy source, familiar, and so forth—has been attempted by a necromancer at some time or another with varying degrees of success.

DEFENSE: Water-based spells will slow a revenant down, but fire spells will consume the revenant entirely. The Haitian *Insandigé* spell was developed to be especially effective against revenants.

SASQUATCH

Gigantopithecus inmensas

FAMILY: *Mammalian*
CLASSIFICATION: *Semi-sapient*
MANIFESTATION: *Corporeal*
PRONUNCIATION: *SAS-kwach*

The sasquatch, or Bigfoot, were the indigenous giants of North America, completely covered in shaggy fur. Standing upright an adult male could reach up to eight feet in height. Mature male sasquatch gain a streak of gray or silver fur on their head and back.

Sasquatch were exterminated in the Magma Wars. There are some cryptozoologists who believe that there are some sasquatch living in the wild, but no credible proof has been forthcoming.

The sasquatch were gentle creatures who were frightened by the cruelty of humankind. Sasquatch had a natural energetic magic that affects the human mind, confusing the human and causing them to forget the encounter with the sasquatch.

Every so often, there are reports of sightings of sasquatch, but none of these have ever been confirmed. Even mundane pranksters have made fake recordings of the sasquatch in an attempt to trick the gullible.

A juvenile sasquatch is called a smallfoot. The word sasquatch is both singular and plural, like sheep or fish. The collective noun for a group of sasquatch is a troop.

It may surprise you to know that when Sasquatch comes up in conversation, I am continually asked if I have yet another expedition planned. No. I do not. The explorer/adventurer market is saturated with my "colleagues" seeking to find these creatures. The sheer number of them, bumbling though they may be, are certain to find the creatures if they do still exist eventually, so I think we'll see a definitive answer to the Sasquatch question within my lifetime.

HABITAT: The sasquatch lived in small family units in dens and caves in the rainforests of Thunderbird Province. The sasquatch was a shy creature, avoiding humans if at all possible. A subspecies of sasquatch known as swamp apes lived in the swamps and everglades of Solaris Province, and a particular breed known as the skunk ape were found there who possessed an olfactory weapon that has become legendary.

BIOLOGY: Sasquatch resembled tall apes with very large feet, often fifteen inches in length or more. The largest known sasquatch foot was twenty four inches in length.

DIET: Sasquatch ate fruit, berries, other human-edible plants, and all manner of insects. It is speculated that sasquatch could eat meat, but they seemed to choose not to.

MAGICAL USES: The pelt of the sasquatch could be made into magical clothing that is naturally resistant to cold. Various internal organs were used for potions and charms. A wand made with sasquatch hair is especially powerful against dark magic.

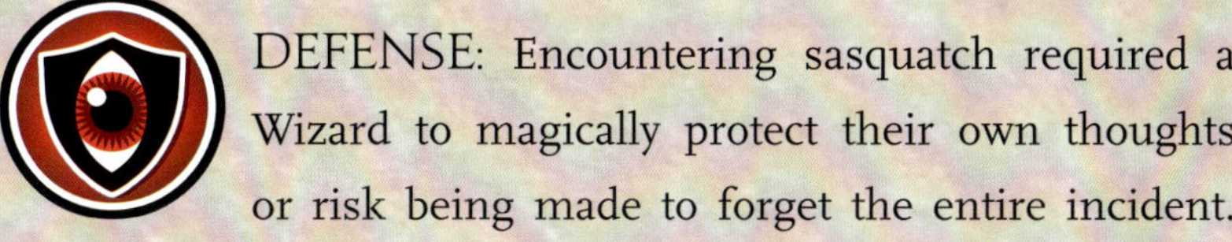

DEFENSE: Encountering sasquatch required a Wizard to magically protect their own thoughts or risk being made to forget the entire incident.

For their incredible size, most sasquatch were not aggressive creatures, and would withdraw from conflict whenever a moment presented itself. Magma War veterans have stated that sasquatch are terrified of being immolated, and should the fur of even one of them be set ablaze would cause all nearby creatures to panic and break ranks. To counter this the creatures learned to douse themselves with water spells before going into battle. If any remaining sasquatch exist, they would likely take every precaution against violence, magical or martial.

SCARECROW

Animus stipulae

Sure a scarecrow is different from a golem, but is it different enough? This whole entry could have been included in golem, which shouldn't have even been part of this book in the first place.

FAMILY: *Animata*
CLASSIFICATION: *Non-sapient*
MANIFESTATION: *Corporeal*
PRONUNCIATION: *SKĀR-krō*

A scarecrow is an artificially animated guardian. They are typically dressed in discarded clothing and may be made out of straw or rags (in which case they are called ragmen). Once brought to life they are set to defend a certain area from specific intruders. Scarecrows get their name from the mundane mannequin set in fields to discourage birds from eating crops, but magical scarecrows may be placed anywhere and instructed to repel any kind of being.

Part of the ritual to make a scarecrow does involve stuffing rags or straw into clothing, but the final product can take any shape the creating Wizard chooses. One thing that remains constant for all scarecrows and ragmen is the more stuffing they possess, the more powerful they are.

Scarecrows are animate, and they may move quite quickly. Those with legs can walk or run, and those without can glide across flat surfaces. Scarecrows are easily defeated physically, but the warding spells they contain cause a violent fright and flight reaction in their targets. This fear attack is especially effective on non-sapient creatures.

When a scarecrow is created, the Wizard breathes life into it. In that breath, the Wizard must tell the scarecrow the general area to be protected and a general description of the creatures it is to repel. For example, a scarecrow on a farm might be told to protect the field from squonks.

Care must be taken when instructing the scarecrow as it follows the letter of the instructions given rather than the intention. For example, an order to guard against all Wizards will turn the scarecrow on its creator, and one to guard against all enemies may mean the scarecrow chases any and all threats indiscriminately. Likewise, the area a scarecrow is given to patrol must be proportionate to its ability to cover the area at any time; given too large an area to patrol, it may not have time to get to its target before the damage is done.

A well-made scarecrow can last about a year or two; a ragman can last a bit longer. The enchanted straw loses its power when it falls out of the scarecrow, and cannot be replaced. Over time, the scarecrow becomes weaker and slower and eventually just becomes a mundane scarecrow. No spell has yet been developed to allow a scarecrow to be refreshed.

There is no such thing as a juvenile scarecrow. The collective noun for a group of scarecrows is a gathering.

HABITAT: Scarecrows are created around the world. They have no natural habitat, although they are most commonly used to defend fields from pests.

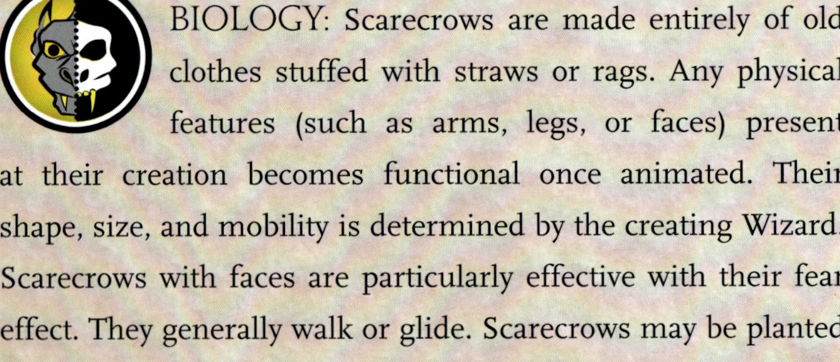

BIOLOGY: Scarecrows are made entirely of old clothes stuffed with straws or rags. Any physical features (such as arms, legs, or faces) present at their creation becomes functional once animated. Their shape, size, and mobility is determined by the creating Wizard. Scarecrows with faces are particularly effective with their fear effect. They generally walk or glide. Scarecrows may be planted in place by a long wooden pole, but often they can lift this pole from the ground and move around at will.

DIET: Scarecrows are animated by the magic of the creating Wizard, and do not require nourishment. Over time, this magic wears out and the scarecrow simply falls apart.

MAGICAL USES: Scarecrows are used as magical guardians, especially against non-sapient pests.

DEFENSE: Fire is especially effective against a scarecrow or ragman. There are spells, such as *Kagànzonge* (Kuh-GAHN-zohn-gay), that can protect you against a scarecrow's fear attacks.

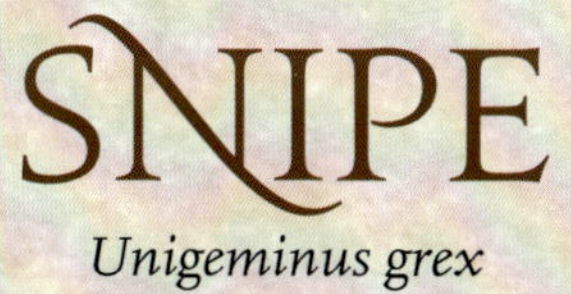
SNIPE
Unigeminus grex

FAMILY: *Arboreal*
CLASSIFICATION: *Non-sapient*
MANIFESTATION: *Corporeal*
PRONUNCIATION: *snīp*

The common snipe is considered a nuisance animal. Snipe are normally invisible, but can be revealed by the use of magic. They appear as small balls of fur with antennae and feet.

Snipe like to inhabit small, dark places, like the corners of disused closets, or inside otherwise empty drawers. In the wild, they can be found under the exposed roots of trees, or in gullies or hollows.

Snipe are harmless themselves, but are one of the main food sources of the common gremlin. In fact, a snipe infestation is usually considered a sign of a much more dreaded gremlin infestation.

A juvenile snipe is called a snipeling. The word snipe is both singular and plural, like sheep or fish. The collective noun for a group of snipe is a swarm.

There is debate among cryptozoologists regarding the taxonomic Family of the snipe. Some claim they are more like plants, and others claim they are more like fungi. Snipe reproduce via spores, which are harmless to other creatures, but make for a powerful magical ingredient, especially in love potions and charms.

These damnable things. Never underestimate the power of the Leeuwendaalder. Drawings of snipe sparked a Magimundi obsession, with youngsters and many adults becoming fixated on the "cuteness" property of these creatures. Before you knew it, finding and capturing snipe and training them as pets became lucrative enough that almost every Cryptozoologist with minimum skills would find it worth their time to gather the things. Snipe themselves didn't help the matter, the bastards, as they got in the act, selectively breaking their invisibility to their favorite humans. "Squeeeee." Then snipe farms started up, which was a catastrophic mistake because the gremlins experienced a similar boom in population what with their favorite food source being so available, and here we are now, facing unheard of levels of gremlins causing countless issues across the Magimundi.

HABITAT: The snipe can be found in temperate, tropical, and subtropical zones. They live in wooded areas, such as jungles or forests. They will occasionally infest a man-made building, usually ones that are either unoccupied or have areas that the inhabitants usually avoid.

BIOLOGY: An adult snipe can grow to about an inch in diameter. Snipe can live up to five or six years in the wild. The antenna of the snipe can grow as long as 6 inches, although this is very rare.

DIET: Snipe are herbivores and eat mosses, grasses, and seeds.

MAGICAL USES: The fur of the snipe is a common alchemical ingredient and is used in many potions. Wands are occasionally created with a snipe antenna core, when an antenna of sufficient length can be found. The spores of the snipe are useful in a wide variety of potions and charms.

DEFENSE: Snipe are essentially harmless, but their spores can be an eye irritant. Flush with water if the spores get in your eyes. Some magi are allergic to snipe fur, but a simple remedy charm can assist with this.

SNOW DRAGON

Draco major glacies

FAMILY: *Reptilian*
CLASSIFICATION: *Para-sapient*
MANIFESTATION: *Corporeal*
PRONUNCIATION: *SNŌ/DRA-gun*

The northernmost reaches of Thunderbird Province are occasionally visited by the exceptionally rare and reclusive snow dragon. Based on limited sightings and drawings, cryptozoologists speculate that the dragon is native to Siberia, but has a migratory range reaching over the polar region into North America. Every few years, ambitious Cryptozoologist Wizards will mount an expedition to "recover" the snow dragon, but as they head north and leave behind the authority of the provinces, they find the independent communities of Wizards of the northern part of the continent will refuse to offer aid or assistance to anyone who has "taken an interest" in the snow dragon. As can be expected, snow dragon expeditions are frequently disastrous, and many have no survivors.

What little we know about the snow dragon has been accumulated from notes recovered from these failed missions. Snow dragons are extremely canny; they have been known to trigger avalanches and strategic collapsing of their cave systems as well as raiding the camps of explorers to ruin or steal their supplies. They also have the ability to alter the sheen of their scales in order to blind their attackers or fade into the snow. However, the snow dragon's most effective defense against too-curious humans is their collaboration with the Wizards who make their homes in the extreme northern regions. These Wizards have been known to point explorers in the wrong direction, spread false rumors about the snow dragons' capabilities, and "accidentally" destroy their tracks.

The main reason I will never mount an expedition for these creatures: sabotage ruins my digestion. A close second is that I dislike being cold.

Owing to a casting taken of a footprint by the 1936 Gutman Expedition—of which there were only two survivors—we can also make the following presumptions and examinations. The footprint was similar in size and depth to those left by elder volcanic dragons of the South Pacific. Assuming that the snow dragon is similar, then the footprint was left by a dragon that was approximately 90 feet long and was over 1,500 years old, making it one of the oldest dragons known to the Magimundi.

Not much else is known about the snow dragons. We do not know with certainty that they are a separate species, or even that there is more than one in existence. It might all be myths and legends, although that seems unlikely. Actual artifacts made from snow dragon parts have been obtained by reputable cryptozoologists, but it cannot be determined if the artifacts came from one dragon or from several different dragons.

Assuming that snow dragons are similar to their more temperate cousins, then they are likely very long lived, possibly with a lifespan of over 1,000 years. They are likely highly intelligent and see themselves as apex predators, eating humans whenever they please. They are almost certainly heavily armored, and proficient in the arts of hunting and killing. They probably have their own language, but can understand the language of humans as well.

Dragons are usually solitary creatures. They sometimes form alliances with the local Wizard community, as the snow dragon has likely done. They can be quite violent and quick to anger and sometimes attack Magimundi communities as well.

Despite being very heavy, dragons are winged creatures and can fly. They use magic to stay aloft, although the smaller dragons can glide for several hundred feet without magic. The volcanic dragons of the South Pacific and the heather dragons of the British Isles can breathe fire. It has been speculated that the snow dragons have some sort of ice or snow breath attack, but this has never been documented.

Known dragons have a life cycle similar to reptiles. They will hatch from a clutch of 3-5 eggs into juveniles, called dragonets, and then will grow into maturity over the course of 90 years. Once they are mature, they leave the family nest and find their own territory. Dragons are very territorial and will fight other dragons or competing predators that attempt to impinge on their territory. Shells from snow dragon eggs have never been found by expeditions or legitimately sold as artifacts, leaving the possibility of a family of dragons open to speculation.

There is a legend among cryptozoologists of a hoard of valuables hidden in the northern wastes of Thunderbird Province watched over by the snow dragons. No evidence of this hoard has ever been brought back by any of the expeditions, but that doesn't seem to stop them from trying.

HABITAT: The snow dragons live in the far north of the Thunderbird Province. As there are no other dragons (save the unique Jersey Devil) native to the Americas, it is presumed that they crossed over from Siberia at some point.

BIOLOGY: Dragons are typically very large reptiles. Their hide is covered with thick, armored scales. They have claws and wings, and can fly using magic. Some species of dragons can breathe fire. It is speculated that the snow dragon can breathe ice or snow.

DIET: Dragons are typically carnivores, with adult dragons eating entire cows, horses, or elk for a meal. As has been shown repeatedly, the snow dragon will feast on humans, especially unwary expedition members.

MAGICAL USES: Very rarely, artifacts made from snow dragon scales, bones, or teeth, do emerge on the market, though these are believed to come from aging snow dragon leavings, and not from any systematic hunting of the creatures. The true properties of snow dragon parts as magical ingredients are unknown or speculative.

DEFENSE: The first and foremost tactic is to go back the way you came. Snow dragons appear to defend their territory through some very clever manipulation of the environment rather than by aggression, so

taking one's leave is the best course. It's presumed that fire or heat spells may be effective, but this remains untested.

SOUCRIANT
(BOO HAG)

Lamia ignis

FAMILY: *Spirit*
CLASSIFICATION: *Semi-sapient*
MANIFESTATION: *Phasic*
PRONUNCIATION: *SŪ-krē-ent*

A soucriant is a shape-shifting vampiric creature with three basic forms. It feeds on the life force of humans while they sleep, extracted in the form of breath or blood.

The first form is a spectral form that takes the shape of a ball of fire. It is not true fire; it does not have any source to combust and can fly freely through the air for moderate distances. The fire of a soucriant is highly unusual: it can be made cool enough to spare the dwellings of its victims or hot enough to cause them second-degree burns. This is the main form of the soucriant when it needs to travel quickly or quietly. This form cannot pass through solid objects, but it can shrink small enough to get through an opening an inch in diameter.

The second form of the soucriant is a fully corporeal manifestation that resembles a human body without skin. The soucriant needs to take this form, which is an intermediate between its fiery form and the third form, to feed. While in this form, the soucriant is fully corporeal and therefore at its most vulnerable. A fully corporeal soucriant cannot fly, but it can still run quickly. Transition between the fiery state and the corporeal is not instantaneous and requires a moment of uninterrupted concentration.

The third form of the soucriant resembles that of a human being. To take this form, the soucriant must be in its skinless form and then don a suit of skin-like clothing, resulting in the appearance of a normal human being. While in this form, the soucriant can mimic human beings, but as they do not possess human intelligence, they try to avoid direct human contact. This form is mostly used to travel long distances and stalk victims unawares. This is also the form that soucriants use during the day.

Soucriants are spirit creatures, and while they may look like humans, they are not intelligent and not fully sapient. They are driven by biological needs to eat and reproduce, not by a guiding intelligence.

They feed exclusively on humans. Experiments have shown that they prefer starvation to feeding on animals, leading to the belief that they require an intelligent life force as food. It is unknown if they could feed on the life force of sapient cryptids such as mermaids or vampires, as experimentation in that area is considered highly unethical. Soucriants must be in their skinless form to feed. Some will feed by drawing blood through the skin, leaving bruises; others feed by inhaling the life force of their victims through the mouth. In either case, the victim remains unconscious through the feeding and will often report terrible nightmares upon awakening.

If a soucriant drains their victim to death, the victim will shed their skin, which the soucriant can take as an additional disguise. Occasionally, however, the soucriant will choose to breathe some of its own life into the empty victim, which creates a new soucriant. This is how soucriants "reproduce."

Soucriants are solitary creatures, each one staking out its own territory. Soucriants tend to have favored victims, and may take one at a time or maintain a circuit of favored victims, choosing a different one each night. If a soucriant is prevented from feeding on a favored victim, it will return several times before becoming frustrated and finally seeking food elsewhere.

The fiery form of the soucriant is called its true form, and takes a good deal of energy to maintain. A soucriant that has not fed cannot turn into its true form. A soucriant usually cannot maintain its true form for more than a few hours, after which it will turn into its skinless form and possibly fall unconscious.

There is no such thing as a juvenile soucriant. A group of soucriants is called a nightmare or a plague. A soucriant can appear as male or female depending on the skin it wears.

HABITAT: Soucriants live in abandoned houses, or in the homes of their killed and skinned victims. Sometimes, they will simply appear as homeless persons that live off the street.

BIOLOGY: Soucriants are spirit beings that take on a physical form to hide and rest during the day. In their true form, they appear as a ball of fire that burns with no source. They can also appear as a skinless form, but it has no internal organs or systems other than bones and muscles. They can also appear as a human being when wearing their suit of skin. When in skinless form, the soucriant has a musculature and bone structure similar to humans; however, they have no true internal organs. They do not breathe, or digest matter. They have no blood that circulates. They do feel pain. The skin used by the sourcriants is not truly part of their bodies and will deteriorate and rot. Soucriants will eventually abandon unusable skin.

DIET: Soucriants feed off of the life force of human beings; it is both a food source and the fuel they need to maintain their fiery state. They must feed each night. If they do not feed for three nights in a row, they will die of starvation.

MAGICAL USES: Soucriants can be trained as familiars as long as the Wizard is willing to feed them human life force. This is looked down upon by the more lawful magi. Potions brewed over the flame of a soucriant in fire-form are extra potent. When treated to prevent rot, muscle fibers of the soucriant can be used as the cores of wands. Their bones can be ground as a spell or potion ingredient. There are rituals which allow magi to wear the skin of a soucriant as a disguise, but these are also frowned upon. The skin is a powerful magical ingredient and can be used wherever human skin would be used, for more potent effects.

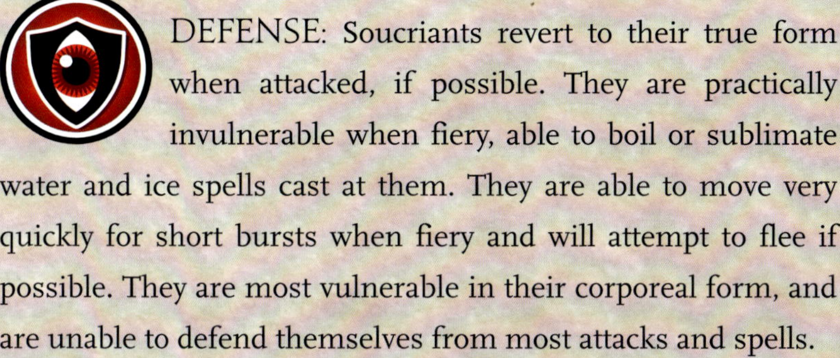

DEFENSE: Soucriants revert to their true form when attacked, if possible. They are practically invulnerable when fiery, able to boil or sublimate water and ice spells cast at them. They are able to move very quickly for short bursts when fiery and will attempt to flee if possible. They are most vulnerable in their corporeal form, and are unable to defend themselves from most attacks and spells.

Soucriants are arithromanic, which means that if they come across a chaotic set of finite items when preparing for feeding, they are compelled to count and/or sort them. The easiest way to keep from being the victim of a soucriant when sleeping is to place a broom upright by your bed, as the soucriant will be compelled to count the bristles. Note that the same system will not work twice in a row. Other systems that work are beans, matches, salt, and sand.

Ahhhh, a creature close to my heart. My fame as a cryptozoologist was cemented by my techniques to capture these creatures, and the Leeuwendaalders from the sale financed my career. Only my most trusted apprentices are taught the spell to flay the false skin from the creature, and the construction of my artifact vacuum prison that prevents the creature from fleeing in their fiery form. I like to think these creatures are afraid of me personally, but they are not quite intelligent enough for this to be true.

SQUONK

Lacrimacorpus dissolvens

FAMILY: *Mammalian*
CLASSIFICATION: *Non-sapient*
MANIFESTATION: *Corporeal*
PRONUNCIATION: *skwonk*

The squonk is a large rodent, usually growing to about 20 inches in length and 20 pounds in weight. It is extremely ugly, with its entire body covered with moles, boils, and pustules. Its skin is loose and ill-fitting and its fur is sparse and stringy, making it look like it has a permanent case of mange. It has long, orange buck-teeth and a permanently mournful expression on its lopsided face.

A squonk produces tears constantly, giving the appearance that it is crying. It even does so in its sleep during which it produces an unpleasant whining sound. Experienced cryptozoologists can track a squonk by the trail of its tears.

The squonk is not an aggressive animal. When cornered, it will dissolve into a puddle of its tears where it will remain until the danger has passed. If the tears are further diluted, or washed away while the squonk is within, it can move with the water and reform later somewhere else. Separating the tears containing the dissolved squonk into smaller pools can kill the squonk, forcing it to remain dissolved in the tears forever.

Squonks are considered vermin and nuisance animals. They are pests to farmers and gardeners, with a special taste for magical herbs, fungi, and other plants. They can get through most fences by dissolving, flowing through a hole in the fence, and reforming afterwards.

Squonks live a solitary life in burrows, only coming into contact with other squonks to mate. Their mating season is in the early spring. The mother will give birth to a litter of 3-8 squinks and will nurse them for a month until they are old enough to go out on their own.

Squonks are nocturnal, and tend to be most active during dusk. They can live in moderately cold weather but will hibernate in northern climes. Squonks' incisors are constantly growing and they need to gnaw on wood to keep them to size.

A juvenile squonk is called a squink. The collective noun for a group of squonks is an impossibility or a grotesqueness.

HABITAT: Squonks typically live alone in an underground burrow. They are native to the eastern coast, ranging as far north as New England and as far south as Florida.

BIOLOGY: Squonks are rodents with typical mammalian biology. The process by which they can dissolve into tears and then reform is not well understood.

DIET: Squonks are herbivores, and especially prefer magical plants.

MAGICAL USES: Squonk fur is not only not useful for magical purposes, it can actually impede the process, producing poor results. Squonk internal organs can be used for spells and charms, but their teeth are especially useful. Their tears can be distilled into a powerful and tasty alcoholic beverage, and are quite useful in a number of potions. However, when the squonk is dissolved in its tears, the whole batch is tainted, making it worthless and giving it an extremely foul taste that can linger on the palate for days. Squonks can be trained as familiars, but they are not popular due to their unpleasant visage, the constant need to clean up their tears, and their propensity to eat magical flora.

DEFENSE: Squonks are not dangerous and will not attack even when cornered. They will, instead, dissolve into a puddle of their tears. It is difficult to keep squonks out of one's garden and they will relentlessly pursue magical crops. Because they can dissolve into a free-flowing liquid, they are not deterred by physical means. There are charms and wards that will keep them out, but these will need to be recast on a regular basis. Squonks are especially vulnerable to ice spells, as the ice will freeze their liquid form into a solid. Wyverns can be trained to hunt squonks, although training is difficult; even wyverns hate the taste of squonk water.

A Wizard suffering a squonk infestation had the clever idea that introducing a small amount of magical acid into the diluted squonk water would serve as an effective means of killing the creature. Wrong. He created the caustic squonk. This creature's tears can dissolve stone and metal. Fortunately, it couldn't mate with regular Squonks and the problem seemed as if it was going to resolve itself as the poor thing approached the end of its lifespan. Unfortunately, some other jerk decided to try to weaponize the creature and recreated the ill-advised experiment on several squonk during the mating season. And wouldn't you know it, the creatures escaped! Aggressive cleanup efforts are under way now to try to contain these creatures. The bright side is that the caustic squonk still thinks and acts like a regular squonk, and is not aggressive even though it has become much more powerful. Wyverns that have been trained to hunt squonks will most assuredly die if they swallow a caustic squonk. And to address the question I am always asked: NO! I HAD NOTHING TO DO WITH THIS! How could you even think that?!

STONECLAD

Homo petrosa

FAMILY: *Humanoid Chimerical*
CLASSIFICATION: *Para-sapient*
MANIFESTATION: *Corporeal*
PRONUNCIATION: *STŌN-klad*

Stoneclads are powerful rock creatures and protectors of the forests, vistas, creatures, and natural elements of the earth. They can be still for long periods of time (up to hundreds of years) and then awaken, lift their heads, stand up, and then move with great swiftness to crush an enemy of nature.

The origin of ancient stoneclads is unknown, but some believe they are part of the mountains themselves and burst free from the rock, creating canyons, arches, and rock formations of enormous size. Today, stoneclads are once-human Wizards who have used powerful magic to transform themselves into large creatures with stone plates for skin. Stoneclads gain access to the elemental power of the earth, and are invulnerable to most attacks. Their power appears to derive from their many talismans.

To become a stoneclad, a Wizard undergoes a grueling ritual that involves embedding an enchanted stone under the skin and branding themself with mystic runes. It appears that some magi choose to become stoneclad for various reasons, but there have been cases of prisoners or other people being captured and taken through the ritual against their will. Since the end of the Magma Wars, forcible conversion to stoneclad has been strictly illegal and is considered shameful and highly unethical. After the Magma Wars, the appearance of new stoneclads has declined greatly.

Any type of stone can be used in the stoneclad ritual, with tougher stones like granite being the most common, although obsidian is also favored. During the ritual process, up to five different stones or gems are embedded into the Wizard's flesh to form talismans. Over the next several decades, the stone will grow until it completely envelopes the Wizard's skin. Once the stone completely covers the skin, the human underneath ceases to exist and the transformation is complete. The talismans remain outwardly visible as part of the finished stoneskin.

The stoneclad's internal biology also changes as the stone spreads. They become stronger and more able to withstand damage. They lose much of their sense of touch, but gain new senses, including being able to sense magnetic fields. Their respiration and digestive systems adapt to their new form, until they no longer need to eat or excrete. It is believed that they obtain nutrients from the elements, including sunlight, rain, and wind.

After becoming a stoneclad, a Wizard will no longer be able to perform magic in the manner to which they were accustomed. The size, quality, and type of talisman will determine the nature of the stoneclad's powers. Some of them are fairly straightforward (rubies grant fire powers; diamonds can grant temporary invisibility), while others are more subtle. A complete list detailing the powers is beyond the scope of this work.

The stoneclad's talismans provide power, but are also their weak spot. The talismans are clearly visible on the stoneclad's dermis and flash when they are used. If they are damaged or removed from the stoneclad, then they lose access to that power. Once a talisman is lost to a stoneclad, it cannot be reattached nor can new talismans be added to a stoneclad after the original ceremony. If the stoneclad loses all of its talismans, it turns into a statue.

Stoneclads are not immortal as commonly thought, though they have an average lifespan of 300-350 years. They regenerate from damage, except for their talismans, and they do not suffer from disease. They do age, however, in a most peculiar way. As the stoneclad ages, the stone in its skin gets progressively thicker until the stoneclad can no longer move and becomes an inanimate statue. There are charms that can slow this process, but it cannot be halted or reversed.

Stoneclad are considered people and are generally accepted into the magical community. As they age, however, they seem to lose more and more of their humanity, thinking and acting in ways that are quite strange. When they start to harden, they will travel off into the wilds to solidify alone. Some Wizards of the Thunderbird Province deliberately become inunnguaq when they solidify. Not all inunnguaq are solidified stoneclad, however. There is a theory of a lost stoneclad graveyard somewhere in the wilderness where the land is littered with statues that were once people, but nobody has ever found evidence of such a thing.

It is possible to turn someone into a stoneclad against their will, although doing so usually kills the victim in the process. It is also possible for a child or adolescent to become a stoneclad, though doing so will permanently fix the child in their current age and size. Many Wizards have experimented on turning animals into stoneclad with no success. There is debate within the cryptozoological community on whether a sapient cryptid could be turned into a stoneclad, although there is no evidence that it has ever happened.

Stoneclad do not reproduce. There is no special term for a child who becomes a stoneclad or a newly created stoneclad. Stoneclads prefer to use the same collective nouns as humans; the collective noun "quarry" is considered offensive as is calling a stoneclad a "golem," which they obviously are not.

*I once asked a Stoneclad why on earth he chose to undergo this process, and the jerk broke my nose! I was just asking a question! I'd still like to know actually. Someone will have to ask for me. There *must* be a reason. I'm sure of it.*

HABITAT: Stoneclads can withstand the elements and have no need for shelter. However, they still prefer to live in simple dwellings within Magimundi communities. Many stoneclad prefer to live with their family and friends, but they do eventually tend to congregate into smaller sub-communities within the Magimundi areas. These communities are often called stonetowns or stone ghettos, although there are those who feel those terms are offensive.

BIOLOGY: Stoneclads have a thick coating of stone as their dermis. Their bones and muscles are changed from human to support the weight of their skin. They still breathe and eat, but they no longer sweat, and have to release heat by panting.

DIET: Stoneclads can consume and digest rocks, which are necessary for their survival, but they still require some animal and vegetable proteins and nutrients, as well. Stoneclads eat larger meals and more often than humans as their metabolism requires more energy to support their weight. However, once a stoneclad has become completely petrified it no longer needs food or nutrients of any kind.

MAGICAL USES: Stoneclads are often employed as guardians or fighters. Some find work as explorers or dealing with other situations that normal humans find too hazardous. The stone skin of a stoneclad, as well as its talismans, seem to have their magical properties attached to the stoneclad and become null-magic items (not useful for any rituals, charms, or potions) when removed. The internal organs of the stoneclad have some magical uses, but they are rare and specialized.

Note: Stoneclad are considered a protected species by the North American Council of Five. They are considered sentient beings with intelligence equal to humans. Harvesting a stoneclad for parts carries with it the same penalties as harvesting a human for parts would.

DEFENSE: Stoneclad are powerful, strong, difficult to damage, and resistant to magic. Their eyes, ears, and open mouth are the most vulnerable parts of them. Their powers are tied to their talismans and removing and/or destroying those talismans will significantly weaken the powers of the stoneclad. Removing or destroying all their talismans will kill the stoneclad. Stoneclad are vulnerable to spells that affect rocks, especially ones that transform them into other forms.

THUNDERBIRD

Skookum azhdarchinae

FAMILY: *Averine*
CLASSIFICATION: *Semi-sapient*
MANIFESTATION: *Corporeal*
PRONUNCIATION: *thun-DER-berd*

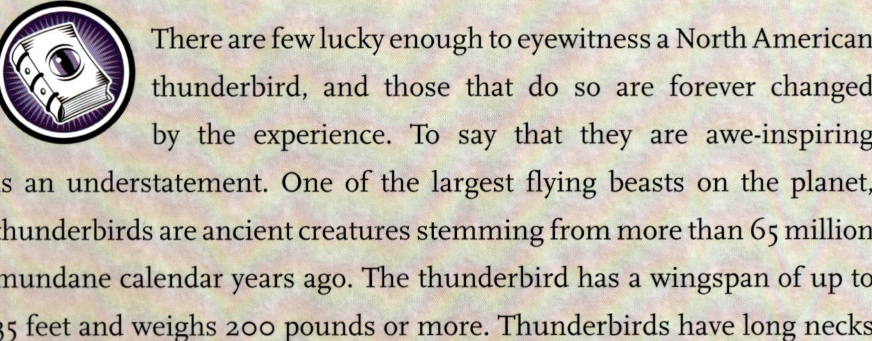

There are few lucky enough to eyewitness a North American thunderbird, and those that do so are forever changed by the experience. To say that they are awe-inspiring is an understatement. One of the largest flying beasts on the planet, thunderbirds are ancient creatures stemming from more than 65 million mundane calendar years ago. The thunderbird has a wingspan of up to 35 feet and weighs 200 pounds or more. Thunderbirds have long necks and protruding hooked beaks lined with tiny teeth. Their prominent eyes have large pupils and appear intelligent, alert, and piercing. Their feathers can be multi-colored, but are predominantly blue, green, black, and silver. Male thunderbirds are also often adorned with red feathers, particularly around the face and neck.

Thunderbirds can conjure great and powerful storms, winds, and weather events. The flap of their enormous wings produces a deafening thunderclap, and a blink of their eyes can produce flashes of lightning. Mature specimens can discharge lightning from their eyes, and the most powerful among them can control the intensity and direction of the lightning, using it as a kind of defense or weapon that immolates or electrocutes an enemy or obstacle. Beating their wings in rapid succession can conjure gusts and gales, or blow rain or hail directionally. Two thunderbirds acting in concert by flying in circles in the same direction can create a tornado or a typhoon, depending on if over land or water. The "El Niño" storm events are believed to be instigated by thunderbirds who appear to be using the storms to alter the migratory patterns of their food sources and drive them toward the shore.

Thunderbirds and mishipeshu, or water panthers, are mortal enemies. In rare instances, thunderbirds and mishipeshu can co-exist in the same geographical area, but only through careful avoidance of each other. Every few years, a cataclysmic battle between thunderbirds and water panthers takes place to establish dominance and redraw territorial lines. These battles result in terrible storms, gale-force winds, torrential rains, flooding, mudslides, and occasionally widespread wildfires sparked by the thunderbird's lightning. When these occur, Magimundi astromancers will use elemental magic to protect their communities, and specially trained forces will head into the heart of the storm to conduct a ritual and offer gifts to the dueling entities.

Thunderbirds are highly respected by the Magimundi, as legend holds that they came to the assistance of their ancestors in the Pacific Northwest by gifting fire to the ancient people. Some believe the origin of magic in humans was also a gift of the thunderbirds millennia ago, though that cannot be corroborated scientifically. They are a protected species by edict of the Council of Five, and should not be harmed or deliberately killed. A dying thunderbird will sing a song that attuned Magimundi astromancers can hear. The song reveals its location and Wizards will mount an expedition to provide hospice care for the bird and to conduct rituals as it crosses over to the Spirit World. The thunderbird then gifts its body to the Wizards, who vow to use it with devotion, care, and ritual purification to create magical potions, poultices, palliatives, artifacts, and art. Due to the long life-span of a thunderbird, many magi have never been part of a Thunderbird Ritual.

Like their much smaller cousin, the raven, thunderbirds can mimic sounds in their environment, including human speech. The song of the thunderbird approaches a low rumble or growl, but with a musical timbre. It often precedes the clap of the thunderbird's wings. Female thunderbirds also make clicking sounds for currently unknown reasons. Thunderbirds tend to mate for life, though male thunderbirds live mostly solitary lives and female thunderbirds congregate in matriarchal societies with delimited roles, shared egg-sitting, and communal fledgling-rearing. Members of bonded pairs communicate over great distances through the rumbling and flashes of light, and one mate can reproduce the call of its partner to summon it to its side.

A juvenile thunderbird is called a fledgling. The collective noun for a group of thunderbirds is a murder. Thunderbirds have a natural lifespan of up to 1000 years.

HABITAT: Due to their great size, thunderbirds require a good deal of space. Because of their propensity for water hunting, most thunderbirds live near the coast or other large bodies of water. They have been found in the high deserts, but are not fond of densely wooded areas due to their inability to maneuver well in the close spaces.

BIOLOGY: Thunderbirds are great birds of prey with a wingspan of up to 35 feet. Their large, pointed, golden beaks are lined with tiny yet razor-sharp teeth. Thunderbird talons are sharp and able to grip the trunks of large trees. The second toe in particular is pointed and dagger-like, and the thunderbird can use it to rake or stab in a fight. Tail feathers are particularly long, lustrous, and colorful and a single feather can be the height of a full-grown mage. Thunderbirds have prominent nares on their large beaks, which allows them to take in large amounts of air. Unlike mammals, thunderbirds have unidirectional airflow through their lungs and heterogeneously partitioned parabronchial lungs. This efficient breathing system allows them to get oxygen even when exhaling, and to be able to breathe at great heights. It is believed that a thunderbird can take a deep breath and remain underwater for as long as an hour, something it does to pursue a mishipeshu retreating to its submarine lair.

DIET: Thunderbirds feed on large marine creatures such as seals, sea lions, dolphins, orca, and wasco. They hunt their prey with their keen eyesight, dive at terrific speeds, plunge into the water, and emerge hundreds of yards later with their kill in the grasp of their enormous dagger-like talons. Thunderbirds prefer to hunt at night, and it is believed that they use a form of echolocation to pinpoint the whereabouts of their intended prey.

MAGICAL USES: Thunderbird bones and feathers are imbued with magical properties that are especially useful in elemental magic. Their giant talons are valued as talismans.

Occasionally, a mage will come across a dropped thunderbird feather, especially after a cataclysmic battle with mishipeshu. After the proper ritual is conducted, the feather may be used to craft an artifact. Cryptozoologists can examine the feather for magical residue and determine if it was plucked forcibly by a mage or shed by the thunderbird itself. Poultices and potions made from their blood or tears are very valuable, but the ingredients are quite rare since they can only be found after a thunderbird dies and gifts its body to the attending Wizards. These ingredients are strictly controlled by the Bureau of Alchemical Ingredients and Reagents Control.

Note: Thunderbirds are a protected species by edict of the Council of Five. The deliberate harming or killing of a thunderbird carries the maximum sentence of life imprisonment in Avernus.

DEFENSE: Thunderbirds do not typically attack humans and the two species rarely have direct contact, with the exception of the death ritual explained above. Should a Wizard come upon a thunderbird nest, they are advised to exit the area immediately as they are in great danger. Thunderbirds are fiercely protective of their young and will exterminate any creature they feel is a threat. To approach a thunderbird directly, the Wizard should drop their wand, staff, or orb, shed their cloak, genuflect, lower their eyes, and hum. If the bird answers their call, they may raise their head, and if the bird nods, they may stand. Thunderbirds will accept gifts from Wizards and seem to have developed a taste for Sockeye Salmon Jerky, which is a kind of candy for them, as the smoking process introducing flavors not found in the wild.

TRIPLE EAGLE

Haliaeetus tricipitem

FAMILY: *Averine*
CLASSIFICATION: *Non-sapient*
MANIFESTATION: *Corporeal*
PRONUNCIATION: *TRI-pel/Ē-gul*

The triple eagle is a three-headed bird of prey native to North America. Its range includes all five Magimundi provinces, from the edge of the Arctic Circle in northern Thunderbird, Mishipeshu and Destiny to the southern reaches of Baja. It is found near large bodies of open water with an abundant food supply and old-growth trees for nesting. It greatly resembles the American bald eagle, save that it has three heads.

There is a legend that the triple eagle was created by a rogue cryptozoologist in the early 1800s as a form of one-upmanship to the European two-headed eagle. However, this is likely to be apocryphal as there are documented sightings of the triple eagle going back at least 500 years.

The triple eagle is an opportunistic feeder whose diet mostly consists of fish, much like the American bald eagle. It lays three eggs at a time and if one of the eggs is damaged or fails to hatch, then the other two inevitably die. It is considered bad luck to disturb a triple eagle nest, and experienced cryptozoologists always carry counter-charms when working with triple eagles.

Furthermore, triple eagles carry three potent forms of divination magic. First, they can be enchanted to give a verbal prophecy on a specific subject, "speaking" the advice from one of their three heads. However, one of the heads always tells the truth, one always lies, and one is occasionally unreliable. It can take experienced astromancers years to determine which of the three heads is always reliable.

Second, the feathers of the triple eagle can be enchanted to dowse, or point to a specific item. The feather must be pure white; no imperfections are allowed. However, the feathers have a limited range, and they must be re-enchanted every fortnight.

Finally, the triple eagle produces pellets like owls, which may be dissected for its contents, which can be used for divination. Again, the pellets may produce true, false, or random information based on which head the pellet was regurgitated from.

The triple headed eagle needs all of its heads to function. If one is removed or incapacitated, the bird will die within hours. They can feed or breathe through any of their heads. They can move their heads independently to allow 360 degree vision.

There was some discussion in the mid-1800s that the triple eagle should be made the official bird of the American Magimundi, much like the bald eagle is the official bird of the United States. This proposal was eventually rejected, although it does resurface now and then.

A juvenile triple eagle is called an eaglet. The collective noun for a group of triple eagles is a convocation.

HABITAT: Triple eagles nest near open bodies of water from which they can catch fish.

BIOLOGY: Triple eagles are essentially three-headed American bald eagles. With the exception of the extra heads, they are biologically identical.

DIET: Triple eagles are opportunistic feeders, catching fish of all kinds when available.

MAGICAL USES: Triple Eagles are highly magical, surprisingly so. Their feathers, pellets, and entire being may be used for divination. Their feathers, heartstrings, and sinews may be used as cores for wands. Their talons may be used to fashion charms to attract fish. Their eyes may be used in charms to allow scrying and other vision-related spells. They put a hex on their nests which causes bad luck to those who disturb them. Their eggs may be used in potions, once cleansed of the bad luck hex. Triple eagles can be used as familiars and are often used to deliver packages.

With my expertise in charms protecting against bad luck, I can always count on a short expedition to triple eagle nests to grab some leavings for components to sell whenever I need some Leeuwendaalders. For the right price, I would be willing to sell some of my charms and annotated maps of the nesting areas.

DEFENSE: A triple eagle will attack with its beaks and talons. Any standard defensive spells will work against them. The triple eagle is not particularly resistant or vulnerable to any specific kind of magic or force, so a mage can use whatever form of offensive spells the mage prefers. Standard countercurses can be employed against the bad luck hexes of the triple eagle's nests.

TUPILAQ

Animus ossum

FAMILY: *Animata*
CLASSIFICATION: *Non-sapient*
MANIFESTATION: *Corporeal*
PRONUNCIATION: *TŪ-pi-lak*

A tupilaq is an animated carving created by mages in the northernmost regions of North America and Greenland. It is traditionally carved from the bones of animals, though in certain disturbing cases, tupilaq have even been made from the remains of children.

The creation of a tupilaq is a private affair and the mages who can make them are quite secretive about the process. The ritual is always performed at night during a new moon. It is believed that the mage must have their face covered so the tupilaq cannot identify them, because a mage possessing greater powers than the tupilaq's creator can turn the tupilaq back against them. It is also believed that the mage performs a ritual endowing the tupilaq with some life energy, although the specifics are unknown. The final step of the ritual is to place the tupilaq in the ocean to allow it to travel to its destination to fulfill its purpose.

A tupilaq is created specifically for purposes of revenge. The creating mage must have been wronged in some way or must be acting on behalf of someone who wishes vengeance. The tupilaq starts its journey in the ocean and makes its way unerringly and without rest to its target, regardless of how far away the target might be. Having found its target, the tupilaq transfers a powerful curse to its victim via a bite, after which it crumbles into dust. The victims of a tupilaq bite invariably die within a day. The tupilaq's bite does not have to break the skin for the curse to be felt by the victim.

Tupilaqs are often carved with several legs and arms and gaping mouths filled with sharp teeth. Their physical form allows them to be trapped, although they are notorious for destroying their cages in pursuit of their goal.

Tupilaqs neither breathe nor eat; their energy comes from the ritual that created them. They do not age or die of natural causes. If they are damaged, the undamaged parts will attempt to continue on their task. If the mage who created the tupilaq dies, the tupilaq will revert into its component parts immediately.

Tupilaqs do not reproduce. There is no such thing as a juvenile tupilaq. The collective noun for a group of tupilaqs is a collection.

Correct. The one sent after me I kept in a glass cage and intended to display it, but it somehow escaped and probably would have gotten me if not for the fact that I was being interrogated by uppity Marshals who "just wanted to ask me some questions," at the time. Luckily, they destroyed it.

HABITAT: Tupilaqs do not have a specific habitat. They are created in the icy north and need to be placed in the sea as part of their creation ritual.

BIOLOGY: Tupilaqs are generally created from animal bone, tooth, or horns, but can also be woven together from sinew, flesh, and hair.

DIET: Tupilaqs do not eat.

MAGICAL USES: A tupilaq has no magical use beyond enacting vengeance.

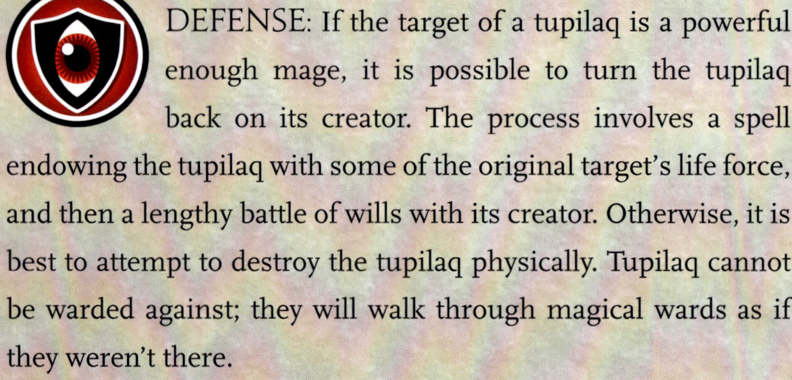

DEFENSE: If the target of a tupilaq is a powerful enough mage, it is possible to turn the tupilaq back on its creator. The process involves a spell endowing the tupilaq with some of the original target's life force, and then a lengthy battle of wills with its creator. Otherwise, it is best to attempt to destroy the tupilaq physically. Tupilaq cannot be warded against; they will walk through magical wards as if they weren't there.

The best defense against a co-opted tupilaq is to publicly admit having made it and why. This will dispel the tupilaq and it will revert back into its lifeless parts. The creators of tupilaqs maintain a link with them and will know if they have

been destroyed, turned back on their creators, or have achieved their goal.

VAMPIRE

Homo vampirus

FAMILY: *Nemort*
CLASSIFICATION: *Para-sapient*
MANIFESTATION: *Corporeal*
PRONUNCIATION: *VAM-pī(ē)re*

Note: Vampire society is especially guarded about revealing secrets; they fear that the revelation of much of the information that would be in this section could allow people to easily hunt and destroy them. Because of this, only limited research has been done on the biology of vampires and a good part of this entry is speculation.

A vampire is a human that has undergone a magical ritual to become something that isn't quite human. Vampires are traditionally considered undead, although there is little evidence for this as vampires do sleep, breathe, and exhibit both a pulse and a heartbeat. They feed on blood, but can also eat and digest traditional human food. Vampires will bleed if wounded, so presumably they have a circulatory system. Vampires do eliminate waste in the normal human ways. It is unknown if vampires are fertile, although it is assumed that while they have the capability to perform the act, vampires do not reproduce sexually.

Instead, vampires create offspring through the drinking of blood. The first bite and draining from a vampire will cause the human to crave being bitten more often. If the cravings are not fulfilled, the human can go mad with desire, suffer terrible withdrawal symptoms, or—in many cases—fully recover from the compulsion.

It is unknown exactly how many feedings a vampire needs to perform in order to convert a human into a vampire. There must be at least one month between the first and final feeding, or else the vampire risks being left with a dead and exsanguinated human.

Vampires can only convert humans into vampires; while they can drink the blood of non-humans, there are no recorded instances of non-human vampires, nor of non-humans developing the same cravings. There is a hotly contested debate on whether humanoid or partially human cryptids, such as fairymaids and mermaids, could theoretically be turned into vampires, but, again, no such instances have been recorded.

Some vampires can cast spells and, in some provinces, are considered full citizens and members of the Magimundi. Magi who become vampires lose their original magical powers and must retrain in order to cast spells.

While vampires can eat and drink normal foodstuffs, they require blood to survive. If a vampire is deprived of blood for a significant length of time, they will enter a frenzied state where they will attack and drain the first creature they come across. If they are sufficiently restrained, a vampire deprived of blood will enter a sort of coma from which they can only be revived by being forcefed blood.

Vampires prefer human blood, either magical or mundane. They gain no nourishment from the blood of other vampires. They can subsist on the blood of other mammals. They can drink non-mammal blood, but do not gain any nourishment from it. Vampires can subsist on the blood of mammalian cryptids, but tend to avoid them as a food source for reasons unknown.

Vampires have a strong allergy and aversion to bright sunlight, which damages and can even destroy them. While in recent years, a topical ointment has been created which allows vampires to walk in daylight without taking damage, most vampires prefer to avoid the sun and will always wear dark glasses in brightly lit areas.

Vampires have the ability to magically heal themselves, although (depending on the type of injury) it may heal itself into a strange configuration. As vampires age, they also change in appearance. Some typical changes include loss of head and body hair, tips of ears becoming pointed, and teeth becoming sharp and pointed. Vampires do age, but they do not die of old age or disease. They can be killed, however; see the section on defense for more information.

There are several sub-species of vampire, each with their own quirks. Some have a natural intolerance to garlic. Some have unusually pale skin, or red eyes. We are hesitant to include this, but it is often asked. Unless ensorceled in some way, vampires cast a normal reflection in mirrors and may enter buildings without invitation. It is believed that these are rumors that have been spread by vampire tribes to sow confusion.

Vampires can, and do, die. The corpse of a younger vampire is identical to that of a non-vampiric human corpse. After vampires reach a certain age, their bodies dissolve into dust when they die.

There is no specific collective noun for vampires. Coven, tribe, clan, and house have all been suggestions. The area where vampires live has in the past been referred to as a ghetto, but that term is now considered pejorative.

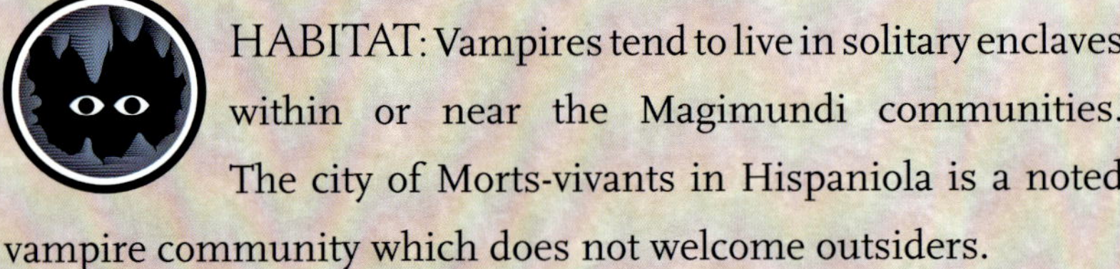

HABITAT: Vampires tend to live in solitary enclaves within or near the Magimundi communities. The city of Morts-vivants in Hispaniola is a noted vampire community which does not welcome outsiders.

BIOLOGY: Vampires seem to have biology identical to non-vampiric humans. Older vampires can exhibit subtle mutations such as paler skin, pointed ears, longer taloned fingers, and the like.

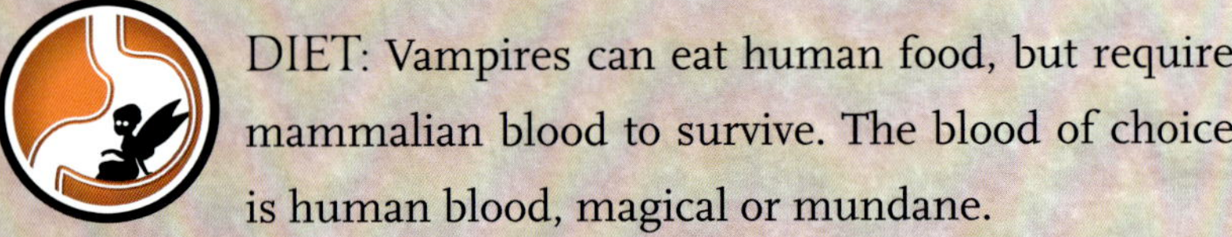

DIET: Vampires can eat human food, but require mammalian blood to survive. The blood of choice is human blood, magical or mundane.

MAGICAL USES: In general, the body parts of vampires can be used identically in spells that require human body parts. Vampire blood is a very potent magical ingredient, but can cause unpredictable side effects in spells that require human blood. The dust of a dead elder vampire is also a potent spell ingredient.

Note: Vampires are considered a protected species by the North American Council of Five. They are considered sentient beings with intelligence equal to humans. Harvesting a vampire for parts carries with it the same penalties as harvesting a human for parts.

DEFENSE: Vampires have a particular hatred of necromancers, and necromantic spells are especially effective against vampires. Vampires can be killed through excessive trauma, but they are able to heal many injuries. They are also especially vulnerable to acid, light-based spells, and electricity.

It's worth noting that there is a farcically disingenuous market for artifacts that "protect against vampires" that is aimed at worried parents for when their children reach that certain age of obsession with the dark and tragic. It is alleged that vampires themselves are profiting from the sales of these fraudulent items. Don't be fooled. I am of course willing to vouch for proprietors who offer the genuine article, so be sure to contact me when little Timmy desires the kiss of immortality.

WAHEELA
(AMAROK)

Canis lupis gigantus

FAMILY: Mammalian
CLASSIFICATION: Non-sapient
MANIFESTATION: Corporeal
PRONUNCIATION: wa-H̄E-la (AM-a-rok)

The waheela or amarok is a very large variety of wolf indigenous to the Pacific Northwest, the northern territories of Canada, and as far east as the upper peninsula of Michigan. A fully grown waheela can stand up to 8 feet high at the shoulder, and weigh over 1,750 pounds.

Waheela closely resemble arctic wolves in shape and coloring, but are much, much larger. They typically have sleek white fur and extremely large and prominent fangs. They are solitary and ferocious hunters; a single waheela could take down a bear or moose with no difficulty. Waheela have a strange way of taking down a beast: they decapitate their prey with a single bite.

Waheela are extremely persistent hunters. They have been known to track their prey for days, even weeks. There is a well-known story of a Mage from the north coming upon the cubs of a waheela and killing them. When their mother returned with a freshly killed reindeer and saw her cubs dead, she tracked the man relentlessly for two months and some 400 miles before she caught him and ripped his head off. She is said to have died of grief afterwards, though hunger and fatigue were more likely to have been the culprits.

A mother waheela will birth a set of 2-3 pups each spring, after mating season. She will raise them for one year, after which they set out on their own. Waheela are solitary creatures; they neither live nor hunt in packs. It is very rare to see a group of waheela, with one singular exception.

Every so often, at a time and place understood only to the waheela, they will come together in a group of least 20, called a tribunal. The largest tribunal on record numbered 57 waheela at once. The waheela will howl to each other and bat at each other, and the younger ones will play fight. However, on some signal the waheela will turn on a member of the group, hunt it and kill it. The reason for this odd behavior is unknown, although there is speculation that it has to do with controlling the spread of disease. The dead waheela is never eaten.

Because of habitat destruction caused by global warming, the waheela is considered to be vulnerable. They are not yet considered to be endangered, but most cryptozoologists fear that its status will change within a matter of years.

The howl of the waheela can cause feelings of angst and loneliness in those that hear it; a bottled waheela cry used as a weapon has been known to terrify and even cause its victims to pass out.

A juvenile waheela is called a cub. A mother with her cubs is referred to as a family. On the rare occurrences that waheela gather together, it is called a tribunal.

HABITAT: The waheela prefers northern areas, from the Pacific Northwest of the United States up to the Arctic Circle. It requires a habitat with a good amount of prey and also some covering.

BIOLOGY: The waheela is, essentially, a very large wolf, with the same biology as an arctic wolf.

DIET: Waheela eat large mammals, such as moose and muskoxen. They are exclusively carnivorous. Unlike smaller wolves, waheela will not scavenge through human garbage. Waheela have also been known to attack domesticated animals such as cows and horses.

MAGICAL Uses: The pelt of the waheela may be fashioned into a cloak that resists cold and allows camouflage in the snow or ice. Waheela fur and internal organs may be used for spells, charms, and potions. The howl of the waheela may be bottled and fashioned into a sonic attack. The teeth of the waheela can be harvested and used in a spell where they are scattered on the ground to form a pack of spectral wolves that can attack on command.

Attempts have been made to domesticate the waheela with mixed success. Some communities in the north have used waheela for transport, riding them bareback. It is possible, although difficult, to turn a waheela into a familiar. The main problem is one of size; the waheela is not an indoor animal.

Keep in mind that these are the same communities that refuse to help snow dragon expeditions, so just because they can do it, does not mean that they'll teach you.

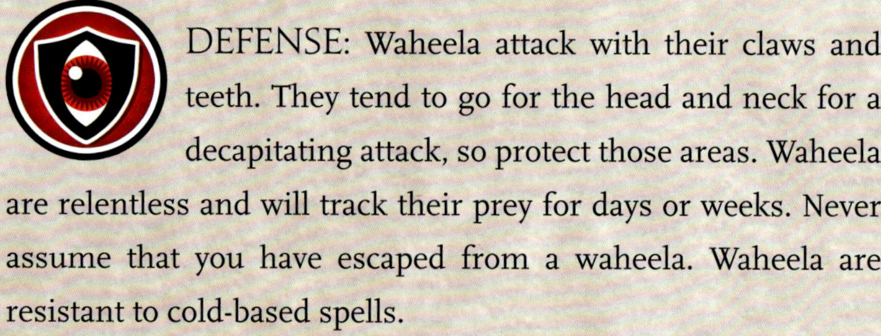

DEFENSE: Waheela attack with their claws and teeth. They tend to go for the head and neck for a decapitating attack, so protect those areas. Waheela are relentless and will track their prey for days or weeks. Never assume that you have escaped from a waheela. Waheela are resistant to cold-based spells.

WAMPUS CAT

Puma hominus

FAMILY: *Chimerical Humanoid/Mammalian*
CLASSIFICATION: *Para-sapient*
MANIFESTATION: *Corporeal*
PRONUNCIATION: *WAM-pus/kat*

A wampus cat is a chimerical creature similar to a centaur, but instead of the body of a horse, it has the body of a large cat connected to the torso and head of a human. It has four paws and a tail as well as two arms and a human head. Wampus cats are as intelligent as people, although they prefer to live in the wild in their own communities and not mix with the Magimundi.

The wampus cats were allies and staunch defenders of the Cherokee people. There is a legend of an especially brave wampus cat that hunted and destroyed Ew'ah, the demon of madness. They can attack with their sharp claws and are also tool-users and apt hand-to-hand fighters. They have a true aim with ranged weapons as well.

Despite the legends of wampus cats being only female, they do exist in both sexes. They are matriarchal, living in large family units ruled by an alpha female. They prefer life in the wild and do not wish to join human communities. They can be friendly to humans, and were allies to the Cherokee people.

Wampus cats have several duplicate sets of internal organs: two hearts, two stomachs, two livers, four lungs, and four kidneys. Their systems are interwoven and branching so that food can be digested in either stomach and they can breathe in both sets of lungs at once. Because of this, they require more food than most animals of their size. An adult wampus cat has an adult-sized human torso connected to an adult-sized panther or puma torso.

Wampus cats are considered carnivorous. Their human stomachs can digest plant matter, but they tend not to consume such things, perhaps because the wampus cat has no control over which stomach will digest its food.

Wampus cats give birth to a small litter of two or three. Occasionally, they will birth a fourth kit, which they call an asegi (ah-SĀ-jē). The asegi has a second feline torso rising from its body in place of any human features, giving it the appearance of two cats attached at the waist. An asegi has six paws and the standard duplicate organs of the wampus cat.

Unlike the normal wampus cat, the asegi possesses only the intelligence and instincts of a typical large feline, such as a puma. Asegi are classified as non-sapient. Many wampus cats will kill their asegi at birth, but some will try to raise it as a typical child. In almost all cases, the asegi becomes a monstrous thing that hunts larger mammals including humans. Seeing an asegi is considered a bad omen, and many Magimundi communities will kill them on sight unless they are being protected by their family.

The existence of the asegi does create a rift in human/wampus cat relations. The wampus cat community is unhappy that the Magimundi consider some of their offspring to be monsters that need to be destroyed, while the leaders of the Magimundi have made it very clear that human-killers will not be tolerated.

Wampus cats prefer forested areas. They will dig dens or sleep in caves. They usually fashion their own weapons, but will also wield weapons obtained from trade or salvage. They live in large family groups, usually with two or three family units living together with a single female leader. Occasionally a wampus cat will be born with magical ability. However, these wampus cats do so at a price. They are rejected by their families who will either shun or attack them if they attempt to reconcile.

Because of this, it is incredibly rare to see a wampus cat as part of the magical community.

A juvenile wampus cat is called a wampus kitten. The collective noun for a group of wampus cats is a pride, with a family unit within the pride being called a family.

A wampus cat outcast named Herbert was my friend and traveling companion for many years. He used a mundane rifle with enchanted bullets, ate tofu, could dual wield wands, and was the smartest and greediest person I ever knew. I miss him terribly even though he stole from me. He died when his cabin caught fire, was lifted into the air by a tornado, and then thrown into a frozen lake. Terrible luck.

HABITAT: Wampus cats tend to live primarily in Solaris nad Mishipeshu provinces, with the largest concentration being around Tennessee. They prefer forested areas with lots of prey. They dislike urbanized areas and will avoid them if at all possible.

BIOLOGY: Wampus cats have dual sets of internal organs, one human and one feline. They can survive if one of the organs is damaged, but they will be unable to hunt well.

DIET: Wampus cats are carnivorous. They hunt and eat small and mid-sized mammals. Only the asegi hunt and eat humans.

MAGICAL USES: Wampus cats will trade with humans, although it can be difficult and laborious to earn their trust. The body parts of a wampus cat can be used for spells and charms. Their fur contains interesting magical properties, and can be fashioned into clothing that allows one to move stealthily about.

Note: Wampus cats are considered a protected species by the North American Council of Five. They are considered sentient beings with intelligence equal to humans. Harvesting a wampus cat for parts carries with it the same penalties as harvesting a human for parts.

This does not apply to the asegi. They can be hunted and harvested and their fur and parts are as useful as that of a normal wampus cat. Some magi have tried to tame the asegi as hunters or guardians or even familiars, but this has inevitably ended in tragedy with the asegi turning on its owner or their family members.

DEFENSE: Wampus cats are formidable hunters and fighters. They are somewhat resistant to magic so especially strong spells are suggested when fighting them. Counter to common belief, wampus cats are excellent climbers and swimmers so climbing a tree or hiding in a river will not keep you safe from a determined wampus cat. Asegi are easily spooked by loud noises, especially explosions. You can often scare off a pursuing asegi with a loud noise.

WASCO

Grampus lupis

WASCO

FAMILY: *Chimerical Mammalian*
CLASSIFICATION: *Non-sapient*
MANIFESTATION: *Corporeal*
PRONUNCIATION: *WAS-kō*

A wasco (also known as a sea wolf) is a strange chimerical creature with the legs, claws, and teeth of a wolf, but the body, tail, and dorsal fin of a dolphin. It is equally comfortable on land or sea.

Wascos have the thick skin of a dolphin and a dolphin's blowhole. They have a great lung capacity and can remain submerged for up to fifteen minutes before coming up to breathe. Wascos have coloration similar to killer whales, with a white belly and a black dorsal area. For that reason, they are often confused with being part killer whale, but the wasco is more closely related to Risso's dolphin (also known as a grampus) than it is to a killer whale.

The magical communities within the Haida people, native to the Pacific Northwest and parts north, have allowed the wasco to be part of their lives. While it was not unheard of for wasco to raid their villages, it was more likely for the wasco to be hunted for a feast, or used for their skills at catching food in the water. There are several stories on record of the Haida people repelling attackers from the sea with their "wasco riders."

Modern day Wizards still command the wasco for transportation or hunting and gathering, but they can use them for political means as well. Ecodefense cryptozoologists have mastered the art of commanding the wasco to disrupt whaling ships, over-fishing, bottom trawling, and to protect the migratory routes of salmon.

Wascos live in social groupings of about 10 to 12 individuals, called pods if they are in the water and packs if they are on land. These groupings change members frequently, with wasco moving from pod to pod as the mood takes them. They hunt as a group, and will come to the aid of other wasco, even those not from their pod.

Occasionally male wasco will fight each other, usually in competition for a mate. Unlike wolves, wasco packs do not have an alpha; they seem to have a more democratic or anarchic system of leadership. Wasco do not have a mating season; gestation tends to last for 13-14 months, with the mother giving birth to 3-5 pups. A wasco reaches maturity in 8 years. The typical lifespan of a wasco in the wild is about 40 years.

Wascos can make clicking noises, like dolphins, and make use of echolocation underwater. They do not vocalize on land, although they have been observed making howling and barking gestures as if they were vocalizing in complete silence. Wascos are extremely clever, and are adept at solving puzzles. Unlike dolphins, they have not been observed using tools in the wild.

A juvenile wasco is called a pup. When on land, a group of wascos is called a pack; when in the sea, a group of wascos is called a pod.

HABITAT: Wascos live in the coastal areas of British Columbia and the Pacific Northwest. They require an area that has both a good amount of cold saltwater and easily accessible land. There is argument between cryptozoologists as to the nature of the wasco. Some claim that the wasco is a sea-dwelling creature that spends time on land; others say it is a land creature that is well adapted for swimming. A wasco does need to sleep on land, but is comfortable spending all its waking moments in the sea.

BIOLOGY: Wascos have the bodies of dolphins, with the legs, teeth, and claws of wolves. Their main internal organs are similar to dolphins.

DIET: Wascos are carnivores. Their diet includes fish and sea mammals, as well as small to moderately-sized land mammals and birds. They are pack hunters, both on land and in the ocean.

MAGICAL USES: Wascos can be commanded to fetch food, and can also be ridden on the land and in the sea (with the proper magical precautions for exposure and breathing). In the past, wascos have been hunted for food, but this has fallen out of favor. Wascos are extremely intelligent creatures and are easily trained. Their claws can be formed into magical talismans that enhance the wearer's fighting prowess. Their teeth and eyes are also used in spells, charms, and potions. Their paw bones can be used as the cores

Riding a wasco is an incredibly invigorating experience, and I have something of a personal affinity for these creatures. Perhaps when I retire from adventuring I will devote myself to the training and care of these handsome beasts.

for wands, which allows for wands that work especially well with water magic.

DEFENSE: Wascos are particularly vulnerable to electrical discharges, and a powerful shock sent into water will drive them to withdraw great distances. This does not mean, however, that they will not circle back to attack on land instead. They have a strong preference for tuna, and the choice fish can be used as a distraction or diversion.

WENDIGO

Homo comedenti

Wendigo, adult

Wendigo, juvenile

WENDIGO

FAMILY: *Nemort*
CLASSIFICATION: *Para-sapient*
MANIFESTATION: *Corporeal*
PRONUNCIATION: *WEN-di-gō*

A wendigo is a supernatural creature created when a human becomes infected by the ethereal parasite, *Toxoplasma wendigum*. The parasite lodges in the brain of the infected mage and causes nightmares and a craving for human flesh. If left unchecked, the parasite will grow in power, feeding from the life force of its host and of the people devoured. The host will become taller and stronger, although no matter how much they eat, they retain their gaunt appearance. Eventually, the host's body will die and leave the corpse under the control of the parasite. That being is known as a wendigo.

Wendigos look like dead humans with sunken eyes and gangly limbs. They are often seven to nine feet tall and extremely powerful. They do not feel pain and are completely immune to cold. Wendigos are extremely hostile and will attack any humans they see on sight.

Wendigos do not live in groups or societies and will generally ignore each other, although they have been known to fight each other for the chance to feed on human flesh. They have no real need to sleep, but they do have periods of quiescence where they appear to rest in caves.

There is no cure once a human being becomes a wendigo, however, healers theorize that if caught early enough in its development, there may be a way to eliminate the parasite. The magical community continues to research and experiment in the hopes of one day delivering a cure. Wendigos are naturally immortal but may be killed through violence.

They are immune to all mundane weapons except fire, and even then only during the day. At night, they are not only resistant to fire, but they have a natural spell resistance making them very difficult to destroy through magical means.

Wendigos are hunted throughout the Mishipeshu Province, usually with fire magic. They are culled in the early spring and late summer during the equinoxes.

HABITAT: Wendigos live in forested areas across the northern midwest Canada. They prefer cold weather and nighttime.

BIOLOGY: A juvenile wendigo looks like a gaunt human between seven and nine feet tall. As they age, they grow more bestial, with the skull elongating and the head becoming more skeletal in appearance, teeth lengthening and claws forming, and finally antlers will grow from their head. Wendigos do not reproduce, but are created as part of the lifecycle of the *Toxoplasma wendigum* parasite. The parasite spreads through the bite of the wendigo, as well as surviving on the dead flesh of humans, which if consumed, will infect the eater.

DIET: Wendigos have an all-consuming appetite for human flesh and will hunt and track their prey to the exclusion of all else.

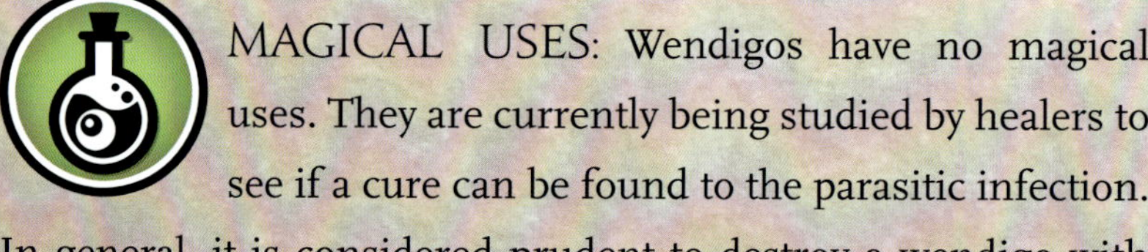

MAGICAL USES: Wendigos have no magical uses. They are currently being studied by healers to see if a cure can be found to the parasitic infection. In general, it is considered prudent to destroy a wendigo with fire as soon as it is discovered.

DEFENSE: Wendigos are fast, strong, cunning, violent, resistant to damage, and can continue fighting after sustaining terrible wounds. Fire and heat attacks are the most effective method of destruction, though the creature will not recoil in fear or panic, even when burning. Successful wendigo hunting parties are reliant on strict discipline and concentrated magical attacks from multiple Wizards, and no hunting party will allow a reckless or uncooperative Wizard to join.

Wendigo antlers can be made into very powerful wands that have a special aptitude for violent spells, but users of these wands will eventually become exposed to toxoplasma wendigum, which is likely why old Castellaw felt the need to omit this fact. Just as healers are researching a cure, artificers are researching a method to handle these wands safely.

WEREWOLF
(LYCAN)

Homo lycanthropus

FAMILY: *Humanoid*
CLASSIFICATION: *Para-sapient*
MANIFESTATION: *Phasic*
PRONUNCIATION: *WĀR-wulf*

A werewolf is a human who has unfortunately been infected by the disease/magical curse of lycanthropy. This provides them with the benefits of improved healing, enhanced senses, resistance to physical damage, and the means of transforming into a large and powerful human-wolf hybrid. The terrible drawback is that under the light of the full moon, the afflicted human will transform into the monstrous werewolf shape, and lose their reason to bestial violence for the duration of the night.

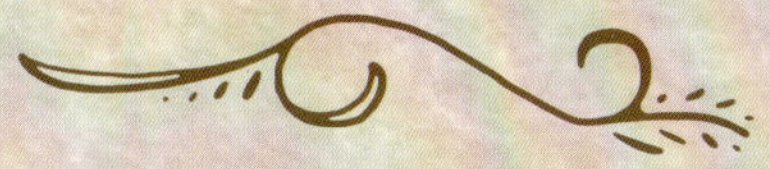

HABITAT: While mostly common to Europe, Werewolves have survived covertly in North America, and can exist anywhere that humans can dwell in the Magimundi, with a preference for forest and wilderness areas.

BIOLOGY: The affliction of lycanthropy is transmitted through the bite or claws of a werewolf. Any wound that draws blood has an estimated 90% infection rate. After an initial bout of fever and nausea, the afflicted will appear to recover, but take notice of the more positive effects. Their skin will develop a more rough texture, teeth may lengthen, and they may suddenly grow thicker facial and body hair. The afflicted will not tend to discover the transformation until the lunar cycle forcibly initiates its first transformation. Afterwards they will find they can transform at will.

The treatment perfected by Peter Romulus effectively allows for an afflicted person to resist the lunar frenzy, so long as they can afford the treatment.

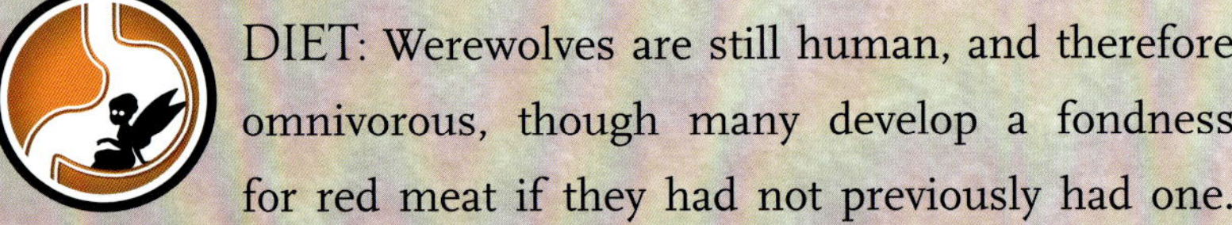

DIET: Werewolves are still human, and therefore omnivorous, though many develop a fondness for red meat if they had not previously had one. Werewolves in a lunar frenzy are basically carnivorous, and may also consume human flesh while in the lunatic state.

MAGICAL USES: Werewolf bone, teeth, and hair have all been used in the creation of powerful curses, or to enhance standard curses.

Note: Werewolves are considered to be human beings by the North American Council of Five. Harvesting a werewolf for parts carries with it the same penalties as harvesting a human.

DEFENSE: Werewolves are particularly vulnerable to weapons made of silver, magical effects from silver artifacts, and spells cast by silver wands. Contrary to speculation, they are not particularly vulnerable to "quicksilver" or silver nitrate. A werewolf in most cases can understand human speech, but cannot talk in their transformed state, so it may be worth attempting to negotiate unless the interaction takes place during the lunar frenzy. In that instance, the mage is best served by aggressively defending their life as escape from a frenzied werewolf is very unlikely.

I am sure it's to Castellaw's shame that his commentary is regularly quoted in defense of Wizards who have slain werewolves because "they feared for their lives." Transform at your own risk, shapeshifters.

WYVERN

Draconis vipera

FAMILY: *Reptilian*
CLASSIFICATION: *Non-sapient*
MANIFESTATION: *Corporeal*
PRONUNCIATION: *WĪ-vurn*

There are no dragons native to the Americas, save possibly for the Jersey Devil. Wyverns are an invasive species brought in by European explorers and settlers. They are a smaller dragon species kept as pets and working animals.

Wyverns have been domesticated by the Magimundi for millennia. They make fearsome hunters, loyal pets, capable steeds, and dutiful guards. There are hundreds of different breeds of wyvern, each with their own distinctive markings. The American Wyvern Association (AWA) keeps a registry of the different breeds and owners can register their wyverns to mark them as purebreds. The AWA sponsors yearly competitions for both working and show wyverns.

Wyverns also exist in the wilds in the Americas, the result of released pets and escaped working animals. They are an invasive species with no real predators and have caused a good deal of harm to the local cryptosystem.

Because of the wide variety of breeds of wyvern it is impossible to say what a typical wyvern looks like. The Great Meerhünt Wyvern can grow as large as 500 lbs and as tall as a fully grown horse. The Teacup Wyvern is a smaller breed and can fit on the palm of your hand, and is usually worn as a shoulder accessory.

Some wyverns have two legs and some have four. All wyverns have reptilian scales and wings, with talons at the end of the wings and on their claws (which may be cropped in accordance with AWA guidelines). Some wyverns do have tufts of feather-like growths. Almost all breeds of wyverns can fly. Some wyverns, such as the Menorviento breed, are bred to race or carry messages quickly. Wyverns tend to have long tails. In some breeds, such as the Wessex Standard, the tail ends in an arrowhead barb.

Even within breeds, there can be a wide variety of markings. Wyverns can be almost any color, with many being mixed, mottled, striped, spotted, reticulated, or with a belly color different from the rest of the body. Wild or unpedigreed wyverns, which are usually a mix of breeds, can appear with even more complicated markings.

Wyverns cannot, in general, breathe fire. The few breeds that can, such as the Marlborough, can only breathe a small flame and cannot hold it for more than few seconds. It is very unusual for unpedigreed wyverns to have this ability at all.

Wyverns are food-motivated and particularly easy to train. Service wyverns have become common to guide the blind, signal the hearing impaired, and perform other functions. Wyverns can be trained to manipulate smaller objects to aid those with mobility difficulties. Some wyverns are trained as emotional support animals, colloquially known as "comfort wyverns."

The AWA recognises 247 different breeds of wyvern. It is beyond the scope of this book to list and describe them all. The authors of this book suggest that those interested in studying more about the domesticated wyvern read the AWA's definitive book on the subject: *The American Wyvern Association's Complete Guide to Wyverns.*

Feral wyverns have spread to almost all parts of the Americas. Scavengers and opportunistic feeders, wyverns are carnivorous, and will eat all manner of mammal, fish, bird, and reptile. In rural areas, wyverns will break into trash and food storage receptacles, so special care has to be made to wyvern-proof the facilities. While wyverns have no real sapience, they are clever problem-solvers and are excellent at opening containers using their claws and teeth.

Feral wyverns mate in the spring and will raise their young during the summer months. By their first autumn, the young are able to fly and hunt on their own, but will still take up to two years to fully mature. Wyverns have a complicated mating ritual, including dancing, bowing, and "singing" to their partners.

Note: Wyverns cannot actually sing, but their vocalizations do sound like strange grumbling birds.

The mating of purebred domesticated wyverns is carefully controlled by their owners. A wyvern will lay 3-5 eggs in a clutch. The eggs will be of different colors and will be warm to the touch. The wyvern that hatches from the egg will have a color scheme that matches the egg.

Wyverns are pack animals and live in groups of about 6-12, plus juveniles. The wyverns will have an alpha, either male or female, who obtained the position by defeating all challengers in combat. Juvenile wyverns usually challenge the alpha when they reach maturity in their second year, just before the mating season.

A just hatched wyvern is called a hatchling; a juvenile wyvern is called a juvenile. The collective noun for a group of wyverns is a legion.

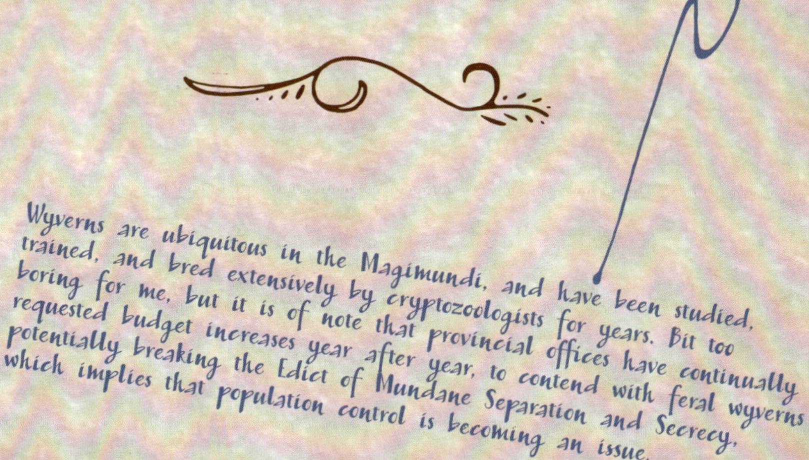

HABITAT: Feral wyverns will build nests in areas of opportunity. The nests are usually at about tree level, but wyvern nests have been found on the ground, and on the roofs of tall buildings. Domesticated wyverns do not need nests, but their owners will usually have some sort of nest-style bed for them.

BIOLOGY: Wyverns are similar to smaller dragons, much like dogs are similar to smaller wolves. They have a scaly hide and wings. Some wyverns have special glands in the throat that allow them to breathe a short burst of flame.

DIET: Wyverns are carnivores, opportunistic predators, and scavengers. They prefer live prey, but will also consume recently killed animals. There are many brands of commercially available wyvern food for sale, although some owners will feed their wyverns table scraps.

MAGICAL USES: Wyverns make excellent guards, messengers, steeds, pets, and familiars. They are fiercely devoted to their owners. Their scales and various organs can be used in spells and charms. Some alchemical formulae require being boiled in wyvern fire to work. The heart strings of a wyvern make excellent wand cores.

DEFENSE: Wyverns will attack with claws and teeth, and sometimes with fire. Unless directed to do so by an owner, the wyvern will save the fire as an attack of last resort. Wyverns are pack hunters and will attack en masse if possible. Wyverns prefer to attack from the air as they are particularly unsteady on their feet. The scales of the wyverns do provide them some armor against normal weapons, and they seem very resistant to electric and fire based spells. They are weakest where the joints of their wings meet their bodies, and are especially susceptible to spells that affect their equilibrium.

NOTES

NOTES

CREDITS

AUTHORS

Mike Young, Maury Brown, Ben Morrow

Humfaeries created by Kickstarter Backer Cassandra Tiensivu

Jesswilee created by Kickstarter Backers Kelley Caspari and Lee Parmenter

Gobwin created by Kickstarter Backer Rob Balder

ILLUSTRATIONS

Creature Illustrations by Ffion Evans

Foxfire Castellaw portrait by Lars Bundvad

GRAPHIC DESIGN

Cover: Anna Kovatcheva

Interior: Erica Schoonmaker

Icons: Browning Porter, Aldie Porter

Layout: Marie Del Rio, Toivo Voll, Maddy Wojdak, Kathryn Lieber

EDITING, PROOFREADING, FACT-CHECKING

Editorial Lead: Anna Yardney

Copyeditors: Sarah Brand, Rhiannon Chiacchiaro, Tara Clapper, Suzanne Molloy, David Neubauer, Lee Parmenter

SPECIAL THANKS

Laura Young

Willow Rose, Austin, and Maria

KICKSTARTER BACKERS

Samma Fagan
Ericka Webster
Liselle Awwal
David Fox-Procenko
Amy Ryan
nachtrabe
Katy Fairbanks
Chris Morrolan Lyden
Kyle Lian
Jenny Underwood
Lucas Gebser
Harry Lewis
Acara
Jessica
Ian Lovecraft
Julie Pike
Anne R Hughes
Melissa Danielle Penner
Casey Hardy
Marc Trottier
Marianya
Peter Svensson
Véra Dalinos
Seamus Reynolds
Nancy
Caitlin Watts
Sara Stiles
Kate Kirby
Thomas Huddleston
Kevin
Kiwi Carranza
Nicole Benson
Monica C Ciuffarin Zupin
Matthew Taylor
Kristen May
Edd
William Coleman
Ian Fabry
stephanie
Andy Erikson
Laura Boylan
Tati
Alainah McDonald
Catherine Stuntebeck
Bliss Lillis
Beth Reed
Dane Higbee
Shoshana Kessock / Phoenix Outlaw
Jennifer Klettke
Tracie
Heather M
Katie Lukens
Sara gessner
Montara Hewgill
Michael Pietrzykowski
Toivo Voll
Hannah Moore
Tom Ryan
Lee Parmenter
Frank Castillo
Tom
Linda Paolino
GearsoulAndrew Wrenn
Paige Liberski
Charon Atchison
Chad Brinkley
Lorne Douglas
Suzanne
Abby Le Voir
Keri Houchin
Aeleen Howard
zack dewar
Tamsin Argent
Ian Struckhoff
Thomas Brudnicki
Sharon Underberg
Trystan Vel
Richard C. White
Alexander Huddleston
Krystal
Darcey Wunker
Garth Sanders
Hallie Cannon
Winston Kou
Jason Woodland
Shea Antoinette

W Ryan Carden
Kendra Tornheim
Jennifer Satterlee
Kate Bakker
Douglas Candano
Andrew Donaldson
Jack D Johnson
Sandiann Devaney
Julie Allard
Uriah Brown
Dianna Halabi
Christina Shirley
Brandon Hare
Korine
Stephen Tyler
Kevin Munn
Makena Seller
Moira Parham
Katherine Hill
Geoffrey Rosen
Philippa bailey
Amanda Schoen
Vanessa Lucy Glenn
Antonio Almonacid
Steve Scibilia
Kristina Stuntebeck
Leah Blue
Madeleine Wojdak
Sarah Brand
Victoria Bukowski
ChristinaS
Michael McDowell
Hannah Howden
Lydia Au
Madeline
Tall_Kat
Josh Conrad
David Donaldson
Izzy
Chvonne Parker
Tara M. Clapper
Caryn L. Johnson
Ganchara
TenChiGin
Katherine Fosso
Kathryn Sarah
Jessica Zarnofsky
Falk Alexander Glade
Scott Boggs
Laurie Rich
Sara Menefee
Talei Ruby
Brittany Miller
Danielle Ziemba
Michael Bromund
Angeline Burton
Nicole Wilkinson
Quintin Scott
Kyle
Bobby Ghaheri
Robert Monkman
Thomas LaMartina
Sean Moulson
Robin Jendryaszek
Jill Racich
Deana Meiners
Melissa Kennedy
Stephen Hiser
Joshua Ethier
Sharon Evans
Morgan Nuncio
Peregrinesflight
Benjamin Schützenhofer
Zachary Daniel
Daniel Tapanes
pamela mazzone
Pierre
Alyssa Staten
Dwight Bishop
Josh Rose
William Sims
Lynn Spearin
Amanda Meuleners
Michael Boyd
Ashley Kaufman
Aimee Smith
MamboDriver
David Kinkead
Chris Lasich
Ffion

Jessie Dettwiler
Jantra
Catherine Wright
Julia Jones
Michael Mears
Amber Feldman
Stephanie DeMane
Lina Hayek
Meriba Hoglund
Craig Fox
Sarah Sloneker
Tyler Dubey
Eric Schiller
Devin Dycio
Jamilet Manzano
Nick Pascarella
Jason J Arne
PunkinPyritz
Mathew Willem Bogaert
You Can Sleep When
You're Dead
Jade
Jacob
Michael Hall
Jared Washburn
Zachary Smith
Cassandra Tiensivu
Ashley Eckert
Lori Corrody
Benjamin L Moseid

Andrew
J. Amaral
Drew Tillman
Troy Wagner
Carl Cunningham
Evan Gautama
Kelley Ross
David Neubauer
Derek Carlson
Jack
Cheryl Sonnenwald
Anthony Houssain
Jessie Clapp
Jason Reid
Kessa
Alan Denton
Charles D Perry
Laurence Wooding
Christopher Stoll
Student_of_Tzu
Jamie Snetsinger
Neil Graham
Hilary McNeill
Daniel Granda
Orli N.
Robert White
Serena Rodriguez
Bill Morefield
Matthew Grover
Tiffany Engle

Patrick Sonnenberg
Anne Holmes
Jessica Enfante
Mike Bermudez
Kathrin Peters
Tabitha Redente
Laoith
Amanda Browning
Beth Bromley
Kyle Ayres
Eric Thompson
Kevin Donovan
Mike
David Corbet
Dana Mirsalis
Jessica Orsini
Elizabeth Robertson
Willhameena Power
Lysander Games
Slade Bolivar Corona
Rochelle Rodrigo-Adams
Tori Zimmerman
Clinton Rickards
Anthony S. Grant
Guillaume Ratté
Bryan
Thomas Murphy
The Bearded One
Ronnie M Weger
Tanya

ohmai
Emily Mahoney
Jess Pestlin
Bryan K. Borgman
Niky Sama
MacKenzie Sullivan
D.A.Dryden
Kaleen Todoroff
brian horton
Thai
Andrew
Maylady Orellana
Moochanoffu
Christopher Tarka
Bridge Mei
Zeke
Denice Clayton
Andrew Chevier
Nick Re
Kirt Dankmyer
Noelle Airo
Millie Taylor
Timothy Kreuter
Sarah Bowman
Judykins
Sheldon Hicks
Michele Mountain
Jen Brown
Veronica Melnick
Reyos Blackwood

Spencer Dewar
Brooke Shedd
R Jennifer Wong
Andrew Oswell
Daniel Abraham
Erin Pierce
Jennifer Ferragut
Destiny Carroll
Keno
Amy Risdal
Vanessa Downing
Willis Schiftner
Danielle Lauzon
Hannah May Lovett
Tasha Turner Lennhoff
Amanda Hubbard
Jeffrey Smith
Jacob Bouvier
Angela Wood
William Dixon
Meredith Muskovich
Lanita D Isbell
Jay Marsh
Pokemontrainerrasi
Valerie Weinstein
KLH
Kaity Hendra
D. Wright
Lauren Hoffman
James N

Dion Desautels
Mario Perez Castillo
Mathyew Smith
Robin Van Hausen
Scott Foy
CC Higgs
Aaron Wescott
Connah Harrison
Devon Barlow
Nicolaj 'Chico' Klitbo
Samantha Dorr
Alice Monaghan
Jacob Blackmon
Joaquin Casares
Alicia Rosebrough
joshua mabie
David Heatherly
Ron Schleimer
Matthew Ruane
Tereza Kulovaná
Reddigan Galli
oaksong
Oneail FX Studios
Lebster
Nick Esposito
Jenny Reed
Kyla
Sean D Harmon
Camden Lamberg
Alissa Erin Murray

Michael Chessher
Angela Basset
Bernard J. McManus
Cory Igneczi
Zachary Derenne
Justin S. Davis
Mark
Fuad Omar
Ben C Schwartz
Frankyjack
John Elson
Cristen Currie
Anthony Hernandez
Kelli Murphy
vile_ettes
Dayna Lanza
Shabir S
Kristine Dietriche
Christina Rowe
Jeffrey Meyer
Coryn Orr
Narjes
Ethiera Pang
Nicole Yousef
Lars Silberg Hansen
Martin J. Manco
Jae Lerer
Brian Shadensack
Daniel Granstrand
Lucille Thompson

Matt Kimery
Andrew Meger
Matt Nixon
Pedro Ziviani
Caroline
Ashley Steele
Matthew Reiber
Brandon Gallant
Kristi Kalis
Kristin Moutrey
Joe Zilvinskis
Luthorne
Anni Thy
Alena Ko inárová
Felix Laurie von
Massenbach
Tri Nguyên
Lilli Bech Jakobsen
Becky Glenn
Àngel Hawkeye Batllori
Patrick Cutno
Skinny Rogers
Jessica Klapperich
Peter Andrews
Curtis Boudreau
Eline Demeyer
Jesper Nielsen
585 Brewing Company
Isabelle Caruso
Christopher Kit Kindred

Astrid Juul-Larsen
Brian Poplin
Niels Ull Harremoës
Heather Hayden
Ginger Stampley
kmusser
Ephiny Hurst
Leslie Johnston
Megan Engelhardt
Simon Khong
Michael G
Ann-Marie Harrigan
Jeremie Fallu
Blake Huffman
Patch Hindle
Rene Williams
Charles Crum Jr.
Ali Kane
Jon Henry
Christoffer Druvgården
Joel Mason
Jo
SideQuest
Michael Lajoie
Rhiannon C.
Andrew Fisher
Lars Colson
Julio Luna
Meckels
Sarah

Kimberly Hrabar
Pat Mason
Kaitlin
Eric Mersmann
Gabe Tanenhaus
Christopher
Liyana Fauzi
Merry Peck
Sherlyn Sum
Joseph Le May
Tarah Butler
Ashley Dunning
Regitse Jensen
Kelley Caspari
Paul Dwyer
Don
Erik
David Erlick
Kyle Saritelli
Kat Swanson
Cynthia Gonsalves
Stephen Tihor
Dan Luxenberg
Pitchayapol
Chunhachatchavalkul
Rohel Terrazas
Miranda Dawn
Chadbourne
Casey O'Connor
Dori Schendell

Rachel Strauss
Sarah Haines
Mary Eaton
Ephraim Mallery
Alex Beckham
Erica Dautel
Suzanne
Sarah Drake
Marc-Antoine
Cheveux Côté
Michael Quell
Gary Robert Criss Jr
Josselin Caron
Bradley Buchanan
Gordon Allbritton
CHAD BOWDEN
Kyle Robison
Rayhne Sinclair
Danny Sligh
not!Player 1
Galena
Santos Montoya
Brandon Carter
James LeMar
Dwalin
Benjamin David
Katherine Crose
Ed Kowalczewski
Theodore Weyna
Greer Hauptman

Ryan Kramlich
Ryan DiSanto
Devin Blystone
M.D.K. Jensen
Emma Andrew
Rob Balder
Joaquin Cogollos
Jen Blaikie
Falos_Zamsash
Caitlin Jane Hughes
Brian Hempel
philosoraptor
Brian Hykes
Grant
Susan. Fulton
Michael Elias
Jakub Saufl
Michael Goldrich
Nicholas Hendley
Travis
Lesley snider
Joel Benay
Christian Holger Pedersen
Brea Paikai
Jeremy The Jinx
Jessica Swiercz
Marco Shessel
Summer Donovan
Patricia Preston
Jeremy Freudenthal

Dominika Kovacova
Amber Lee Peace
Oriana Kramer Almquist
Bellehound
Matt Britt
Suzy Pop
lcnyoung
Jessica Brown
Andrew Leisz
Megan Coppock
Sewicked
Norm Welsh
Michael Loewinger
Caitlin Ferguson
Michelle Saiz
Kevin Legault
Scott Myrden
Carmen Marin
Scott Early
Patrick Spence
John Bowen
Micah Miller
Michael Anderson
mats
Mathias Christensen
Ken Herbert
Tucker Le
Templeton Klos
Eärendil Enbuske
Daniel Feldmann
Katherine Rosland
Chuck Parker
Mark Nielsen
MKirkland
Sergey Anikushin
Scott Forloine
Jeffrey Joiner
jimcripps
Christopher Amherst
Tiffany Christensen
Andrew Bancroft
MJ
N. Frances Moritz
Roisin McCormac
Wyatt Beougher
Edward Nycz Jr.
Richard Burns
Charlotte Braxton
Peter
Matthew Sullins
Tiffany Kerr
Frank Beres
Eduard Lukhmanov
Laura Sirola
Mike Presley
Michael J. Matlock IV
Alexander Gudenau
Molly Jættebarn

COMING SOON

MAGI MUNDI™

BOOK ONE: THE CURSED COVENANT

arriving early 2017

New World
Magischola
M
OMNES AB
OMNIBUS
DISCAMUS
© LearnLarp, LLC

ISBN 9781945097003

52499 >

9 781945 097003